ROMANCING THE WORLD

ROMANCING THE WORLD

A BIOGRAPHY OF

IL DIVO

ALLEGRA ROSSI

Copyright © Allegra Rossi 2005

The right of Allegra Rossi to be identified as the author of this work has been asserted
by her in accordance with the Copyright, Designs and Patents Act 1988.

First published in hardback in Great Britain in 2005 by Orion Books
an imprint of the Orion Publishing Group Ltd
Orion House, 5 Upper St Martin's Lane,
London WC2H 9EA

10 9 8 7 6 5 4 3 2 1

A CIP catalogue record for this book is available from the British Library.

ISBN: 0 75287 519 1

Design by www.carrstudio.co.uk
Printed in Great Britain by Clays Ltd, St Ives plc

Every effort has been made to fulfil requirements with regard to reproducing copyright material.
The author and publisher will be glad to rectify any omissions at the earliest opportunity.

www.orionbooks.co.uk

Contents

'You don't merely listen to Il Divo; the music connects with your soul'

IL DIVO

An Introduction

CLASSICAL
WITH CHARISMA

'For me, [Il Divo] was the best thing I had ever heard.'
Simon Cowell

Every great story starts with a mystery, and the legend of Il Divo is no exception. Il Divo are not just any four young men gifted with masculine, passionate voices. More than a boy band, more than a quartet of opera singers, more than four faces the cameras love, the sum of Il Divo is greater than its parts. The group channels the power vested in music by the human soul, making women weak at the knees and grown men cry. And, as an added bonus, these talented male singers are also easy on the eye – groomed and dressed to fit an elegant image of musical fantasy.

Il Divo, at the time of writing, have had a number one album in twelve countries and a top five album in twenty-five countries, going platinum in the USA, the UK, Canada, Ireland, Australia and New Zealand as well as Hong Kong, Spain and France. With over 4 million records sold, they have proved that the

'While virtually anyone can sing pop,
opera still demands training
and dedication'

world is ready for their superior combination of vocal strength, elegant presentation and emotional connection. You don't merely listen to Il Divo: the music connects with your soul.

There are two separate accounts of how this singing phenomenon came into being. One tale was told by the baritone of the group, Carlos Marin, in 2005 during an interview with Canadian *Elle*. It seems that Simon Cowell was watching a performance of The Three Tenors on TV and was inspired by the 'popera' genre, to the point where he formed the idea of finding new singers for what was to become an operatic supergroup. The second story was told in that same year by Cowell himself to Katie Couric, the presenter of the extremely popular American talk show *Today*. Here, Cowell said he was watching an episode of *The Sopranos* in which Tony Soprano's wife, Carmela, was listening to Sarah Brightman and Andrea Bocelli in a duet singing 'Time To Say Goodbye' ('Con Te Partiro'). This single got to number two in the British singles charts in May 1996 and remained there for fourteen weeks. Cowell admitted, however, that almost anyone could have predicted the success of the 'popera' cross-over. The single – 'Time To Say Goodbye' – became the biggest-selling single in Germany in 1997, where it stayed on the charts for an unthinkable period of ninety-eight weeks, selling an incredible 2.5 million copies.

In fact, within one short year of the release of their debut self-titled CD, Il Divo were to outsell Bocelli and Brightman. But first Cowell had to find the four men who could fulfil his dream of creating a band that straddled both the worlds of opera and pop and appealed to both men and women, and young and old alike. Whatever really happened on that fateful day sometime in 2001, the result has been a staggeringly successful popera group that proves elegance, quality and emotion still count in the world of music.

Because of the training involved in operatic singing, most non-chorus performers are trained as soloists – and so it is not surprising that Il Divo is a group that didn't form itself. Soloists, by their very nature, do not seek to form professional alliances with other soloists. Even with the great popularity of The Three Tenors, Plácido Domingo, José Carreras and Luciano Pavarotti only ever united for three event-related recordings.

It was to take two years for Il Divo to take shape as a group. Although it may seem an obvious formula – discover four good-looking men who can sing, stick them in suits and get them to perform – finding the perfect balance of four voices and four distinct yet winning personalities was a harder task than you might imagine. Simon Cowell has admitted in a UK newspaper that, 'I don't know that I'd have taken an ugly one.' Cowell is, after all, noted for his honesty.

'Il Divo is the ultimate in sophisticated music made readily available and accessible'

Known as 'the Caustic Critic' and Cowell 'the Scowl', television's *Pop Idol* and *American Idol* have thrown Simon Cowell into the limelight as the world's meanest man. Public opinion notwithstanding, he has a vital role as one of popular music's greatest Svengalis. He may come across as vile, opinionated and vocal, but he also has a wealth of experience of the music business and the talent to develop any potential he discovers – two things money can't buy. Cowell is one of only a few people who seem to have the magic touch: he knows how to choose music that people actually want to hear and, of course, buy. No wonder that on the *American Idol* show, his comments are the ones that the participants cling to the most. They may not like his abrupt style, his cutting remarks or even his face, but this is a man who needs to suffer no fools – not with a track record like his.

Born in England in October 1959, Cowell's career in music started when he was twenty, on joining EMI Music Publishing. In 1989 he was offered a position as the artists and repertoire consultant for BMG. In an industry where burnout and failure are the norm, Cowell's list of successes includes many massive hit acts such as Sonia, Five, Westlife and Curiosity Killed the Cat. Along with his lesser-known TV work behind the scenes, Cowell also had a hand in bringing the sonic talents of the Teletubbies to a Christmas number one. But Cowell himself admits that the singing duo Robson and Jerome was a turning point in how he saw new musical groups coming together. With sales of more than 25 million albums, more than seventy top thirty hits and nearly twenty number one singles to his credit, via his creations, clearly Cowell is a man who not only knows the music industry but is also that rare thing: a long-game trendsetter.

Having decided a marriage of opera and pop music was the next big thing, in 2001 Cowell sent talent scouts out across the world to find the singers for his new supergroup. Cowell knew he would not find the kind of trained voices he needed on some amateur talent contest; he needed four experienced singers who knew exactly what they were about. The rest, as they say, is history, for the four men the scouts returned with proved perfect for Cowell's plans – there were no second bests and no replacements: Urs Buhler, Carlos Marin, Sébastien Izambard and David Miller were destined to be Il Divo. With the ability to work together as a quartet, they are all singers in their own right whose voices have joined with pop and more traditional songs to bring light opera to a modern age.

Il Divo is the ultimate in sophisticated music made readily accessible and enjoyable, the only classical group to embrace all aspects of pop culture – the screaming fans, the number one hits, the TV talk shows, the tours, the limousines and all that fame allows – without compromising their hard-won skills. They can and do successfully compete with pop music, proving that the skills of classical singing are not only recognised but appreciated by audiences the world over. In fact, according to one opera 'philosopher', opera singing affects the perceptions of its listeners in ways that are unknown to other forms of music; the effects of a sustained, fully developed human voice are almost otherworldly.

Considering the power of the trained voice, it is no surprise that Il Divo captures the hearts and minds of opera and pop music fans alike. The group brings the world of opera to people who firmly believe that opera is not for them.

Classical music – and most specifically operatic music – had its heyday in the seventeenth and eighteenth centuries. Then, because it was the predominate form of public entertainment, opera singers became huge stars, each with their own band of passionate fans. Although opera pieces were originally sung in Italian, opera's popularity ensured that it was soon written and sung in other European languages such as French, English and German – a fact reflected in the nationalities of the members of Il Divo. However, over time light opera gave way to music hall entertainment, and when that waned, jazz came to the fore, spawning rock and pop as we now know it. Despite its value as a musical training technique and the skill required for its proper performance, classical singing was relegated to church choirs and orchestras – formal organisations in an increasingly informal world.

Now, however, classical music is on a comeback trail. The unforgettable use of 'Nessun Dorma' during the 1990 World Cup spawned a thirst for music that isn't rock 'n' roll but is still powerful. In 2005 Michael Quinn, the deputy editor of *Gramophone* magazine, told the *Sunday Telegraph* that the interest shown in classical music by record companies was a trend waiting to happen. 'I think the classical crossover genre has a longer history than people realise . . . What is new, however, is the willingness of record labels to invest in these acts.' This is reflected in the popularity of such artists as Vanessa Mae and Russell Watson and the recent signing of Bond, an all-female troupe, as well as G4, the stars of TV's *X Factor*. And, of course, one of its best proponents is a certain poperatic quartet called Il Divo.

The operatic voice is different from most other forms of singing in that it began before electronic amplification. In the early days, singers had to rely on their own vocal projection to make sure all of the audience could hear them, and this includes the use of what are known as 'resonators'. The operatic technique requires the singer to consciously engage parts of their mouth and throat such as the palate, pharynx and larynx to produce the strong, clear, unencumbered voice that is normally associated with opera. Recordings of singers from the last century show how much vocal styles have changed. While virtually anyone can sing pop – according to some experts it is very near to normal speaking – opera still demands training and dedication.

Popular music, apart from being fun to listen to, is often the soundtrack to our lives. If our lives are a movie and we're the stars, the music we hear is certainly the soundtrack – a sonic indicator of our emotions, our hopes and dreams. Popular music of all kinds is part of our culture, an art form that reflects our daily reality.

True opera voices – such as that of Maria Callas or Plácido Domingo – are certainly stronger and richer than those in Il Divo, but popera can introduce new listeners to more hardcore opera and classical singing. It is often the case that one musical genre will lead off into another; someone who loves soul may learn to love jazz. People who have never heard live classical orchestral music may suddenly find themselves hooked after hearing Chopin or Mozart played on electronic instruments as part of a film score. Watching Il Divo is not the same experience as seeing a full-scale opera, but what the group provides is an accessible taster to that world. They understand the visceral power of operatic singing and use it to full effect. These are not four men who merely sing: they emote and you feel it through your body – not just through your ears.

Although it may be hard for non-opera experts to tell which member of the band is singing which parts on the first album, listening carefully to the songs over and over exposes the distinctive vocal stylings of each of the singers. Both David and Urs have full, round, beautifully schooled operatic voices – easily good enough for the stage. Carlos's mahogany-toned baritone is the easiest to pick out from the weave of voices; his is the rich, mellow voice that nevertheless thrives in an upper register, while Sébastien's provides the crucial pop style. You can hear that rich mix of all four voices on the single 'Regresa A Mi'. It was no accident that this was the song Il Divo sang when they made their first ever broadcast appearance on *Parkinson* on 18 September 2004 – Simon Cowell knew its lush tones and climactic choruses would have an instant appeal for listeners hungry for songs with emotional depth and breadth. And so it proved to be. That appearance was to whet the appetite of the public to know more about this beautiful music and much more about the four charismatic men performing it.

'These are not four men who merely sing: they emote and you feel it through your body'

IL DIVO

DAVID MILLER

'The opera world does not want its art disturbed.
To them, it's like taking Mona Lisa and dressing her
up in a mini-skirt.' David Miller

David Miller is the American limb of Il Divo. The tallest member of the troupe, David was born on 14 April 1973 in San Diego and raised in Littleton, Colorado. Of his early years, he says, 'In high school, I got roped into musicals because they needed guys. I played Rooster in *Annie* and Noah in *Two by Two*. My voice teacher recommended that I study with Richard Miller (no relation) at Oberlin. And the show that inspired me to sing opera was *La Bohème*. My roommate put on a recording of [Luciano] Pavarotti and [Mirella] Freni. "Wow!" I thought, "I wanna sing that high C and hold it twice as long." Even though there's so much pressure in opera, I decided to go for it because my dad always told me, "Better to shoot for the stars and miss, than shoot for a pile of cows – and be on target." '

The tenor, whose eyes are blue-grey, graduated from Oberlin, a music conservatory that some performers prefer over the famous American music school Julliard. There David took a Bachelor degree in Vocal Performance, which included theory, ear training, music history and piano as well as Italian, German, French and diction lessons. David shone in his lessons, according to Professor Richard Miller, who said of David's schooling period, '[He] was a pleasure to teach. His growth during his Oberlin years brought me much personal satisfaction. He has the essential parts of the professional performance package: excellent voice, fine technique, interpretative and stage abilities, and solid musicianship.'

Singers, unlike musicians, sometimes mature later and therefore often need to do graduate work, becoming apprentices to further their talents and secure skills that will enable them to have a career singing professionally. David chose to take a Masters degree in Opera Theatre at the college, which, with its relatively small graduate body (there are only about 100 students majoring in Voice at any one time), offers performing opportunities rarely found elsewhere. Although David had initially wanted to go on Broadway, singing in the chorus of *La Bohème* in his second year at Oberlin changed his mind and the course of his career. 'I decided that one day, I wanted to be Rodolfo. I told Richard, who laughed me out of the io. But I kept at it. At the end of that year, when I took 'Che Gelida Manina' to him, he said, "OK, you've been whining about it all year, go ahead." After I sang it, he said, "It's your calling." ' Obviously, the mix of David's raw talent, determination and the school's structure honed him into the voice and the performer he is now, thrilling us as the bright, strong voice of Il Divo. In *Playbill*'s Celebrity Buzz: Leading Men column of January 2003, Wayman Wong listed among his seven favourite musical moments of 2002 'David Miller, "Che Gelida Manina", *La Bohème*, Broadway Theatre'. So practice, in David's case, made perfect.

Before Il Divo, David had had a base in New York for a decade; his career had already spanned forty-five different operatic and musical theatre parts. Ever since his astonishing debut in 1997 with Washington Opera's production of *La Traviata*, playing Alfredo, David was one of the finest young American tenors on the operatic scene. A list of his roles comprises classic after classic, each noted for a variety of challenges and difficulties for the best of tenors. In 1999 he took on the part of Edgardo in the opera *Lucia di Lammermoor* at Festival Opera. The next year, he was in the lead role in *Werther*. (In fact, his decision not to return to Festival Opera, so that he could join Il Divo, meant that two singers had to

replace him.) David also sang in *Manon Lescaut* in Trieste and was, at one point, a member of the Pittsburgh Opera Center. He's worked in America, Australia and Europe – including a stint as the expressive Tony in *West Side Story* at La Scala in Milan.

David told *People* magazine in June 2005 that in high school he was considered a geek – singing in the choir, being a good student and liking drama. 'I was somewhat of an oddball.' Now, of course, the tables have turned. Nicknamed 'the stud tenor' by the *San Francisco Examiner*, David is more than just a superb operatic voice in a long, model frame. David's face is expressive; when he sings, his eyes open wide, his jaw and all his facial muscles move to form the sounds, getting the pitch and volume perfect. Working on the stage rather than in the recording or television studio, and therefore needing to be seen by those in the back row, David's face and body language come into their own.

He's a man of many parts and many different tastes. He's a film fan and loves Monty Python, but his favourite movie is *Star Wars*. As he once put it, 'I'm a big fan and my girlfriend calls it my religion.' Some say he is a risk-taker too, with hobbies that include snowboarding and motorcycling. In terms of music, he loves techno and adores drum 'n' bass. Give him Eminem or Björk or The Prodigy any day and he's happy; in fact, when it comes to music, the more hardcore it is, the more he likes it. 'Opera is what I do, but it's not what I am. I don't listen to it when I'm home. I like hard rock, alternative bands, techno. Korn, Third Eye Blind, System of a Down. One of my hobbies is deejaying . . . and I actually [can be] more nervous about that than singing.' Before Il Divo, David considered opera part of his musical roots and despite the musical theatre taking hold – and now the glorious pop of Il Divo – he used to sing opera in the privacy of his own home. Whether he still does 'crack open a score and sing through one of my shows' is doubtful. The group's touring and recording schedule just won't allow time for it. In fact, he's admitted in other interviews that he partied more when he was singing opera than at any time being with Il Divo.

David's early career was flourishing. One of its high points was the applause for his role in Baz Luhrmann's production of Puccini's *La Bohème*, which opened on Broadway in December 2003. Oberlin Conservatory proudly took note that their 1995 graduate was in the elaborate, crowd-pleasing production but also that he had been in *Vogue* and immortalised by the famous caricature artist Al Hirschfeld. Luhrmann, better known as the director of ground-breaking films such as *Romeo & Juliet*, *Strictly Ballroom* and *Moulin Rouge!*, is known to have an eye and an ear for the dramatic. The selection of David Miller in the vital role of Rodolfo was in keeping with Luhrmann's trademark quality and flourish, but was also a ringing endorsement of David's incredibly strong, clear voice – and the fact that the singer can emote very well on stage.

David found the Broadway experience more satisfying than he ever thought possible. In the same interview with Wong for *Playbill*, he said, 'It's been a whirlwind. It's surreal. It's surpassed all my expectations. Two years ago, when auditions first started, I thought, "Broadway opera? What the hell is this?" But I also thought, "This could be really cool!" Omigod! In the seventeenth and eighteenth centuries this art form produced the rock stars of their day, and now it's become this tradition of stereotypes of large people screaming their guts out. This [*La Bohème*] was an amazing chance to bring some youth and vitality to it.'

According to David, Luhrmann 'approaches everything from the standpoint of truth. Baz strips away all the "opera acting", all the Italian, and gets to the words and what you're trying to convey. To Baz, the voice is the last layer of the performance, not the first – unlike opera, where the emphasis is on the voice, and if you can act, it's a bonus. But Baz believes, as I do, that you have to connect with what you're singing and the other people on stage. If you want pure vocal tone, go to a recital. What's the difference between going to an opera and a recital? The drama.'

The way Luhrmann cast *La Bohème*, with young and sexy singers, put New York into a tizzy. But David took it in his stride, saying that yes, the show was sexy, but what wouldn't be sexy with a story about a handful of beautiful young people who fall in love with each other in Paris? For David, the experience of *La Bohème* was amazing not only for the story itself and the opportunity but also because he was given time to rehearse. 'In most opera companies, you have only two weeks to rehearse and limited tech and orchestra time. Here, we rehearsed for two months and explored the text before we even went into the theatre.'

Sharing the role of Rodolfo with three other singers – Alfred Boe, Adrian Dwyer and Victor Robertson – wasn't an issue with the young tenor. 'The cast rotation keeps it fresh and interesting for everyone. I couldn't imagine being in a single cast of, say, *Cats*, and doing it for ten years or whatever. I'd want someone to claw my eyeballs out. But every time I do *La Bohème*, I always find something new.'

'What we've created is something completely new and extremely exciting'

'David Miller is a superlative tenor and an actor of astonishing range, equally comfortable as enraptured lover or clown'
Variety

And so he did. David, all six foot three of him singing in Italian, gave performances that grabbed critics by the lapels. Michael Feingold of New York City's *Village Voice* took a swipe at Luhrmann's high profile and the fact that film producers Bob and Harvey Weinstein were onboard to supply financial clout, but admitted that the money did allow the director to find an exceptional voice in David Miller: 'Luhrmann's chief advantage is simply that his international stature and movie money allow him to sift through a worldful of young singers for his troupe. He's found some choice artists. In the two casts I heard, David Miller and Ekaterina Solovyeva were a vocally rich Rodolfo and Mimi.'

Critic Sharon Perlmutter said, 'The company is first rate. David Miller, the opening night Rodolfo (up to four actors rotate through each principal role), has a lovely, passionate tenor that even this opera neophyte recognised as being of superior quality.' Joel Hirschorn wrote in *Variety* on 20 January 2004 that, from the two performances he viewed, 'David Miller is a superlative tenor and an actor of astonishing range, equally comfortable as enraptured lover or clown.' A critic from the Associated Press gushed, 'Miller heartbreakingly captures a boyish fellow suddenly turned grown-up in grief.' The *New York Times* critic Ben Brantley commented that 'the stars of this *Bohème* may be as pretty as Calvin Klein models photographed by Avedon … their voices, for the most part, match their faces . . . I have never seen an opera in which movement seems so spontaneous or so particular to each individual.' If Baz Luhrmann's *La Bohème* was said to have revived opera for Broadway, David had a hand in that endeavour. One night he performed in a theatre stuffed with the likes of Nicole Kidman, Sandra Bullock, Leonardo DiCaprio and Hugh Grant. Working with an international cast, which included Daniel Okulitch (another Oberlin graduate), Tim Jerome, Janinah Burnett and Wei Huang, David was able to garner even more experience with different cultures and languages – something that would stand him in good stead for his upcoming gig with Il Divo. He can speak a little Japanese, and he can, of course, sing in Italian and Spanish as well as English when required.

Joining Il Divo was as much of an adventure for David as it was for the other members of the supergroup. Of course, he had heard that hundreds of singers auditioned for his role, but he says he didn't know Cowell was behind the auditions until he actually got the gig. 'I was told, "Simon wants to meet you." "Simon who?" "Simon Cowell." I said, "Oh, crap. This is gonna be a lot more high-profile than I thought." ' He was told that Il Divo's fans would be of a certain type, and was surprised to find out later that in fact they are more diverse than anyone could have predicted. 'Initially, they thought our fanbase would be just housewives,' David said, 'but it runs from thirteen to eighty-five on our website, and we have a lot of male fans too.'

Simon Cowell loved the idea of artists like Andrea Bocelli and The Three Tenors – their power, their dramatic attraction and their sound – but he really hated the music they performed. Hence his idea for auditioning just the right performers for this operatic pop magic act – no women, because, as Cowell was once quoted as saying, 'women singers sound squeaky'.

Like a script for a film, the music had to be just right. 'We don't want to take anything from the classical repertoire, to alter things that purists might come down on,' David says. But when the Diane Warren-crafted Toni Braxton hit 'Unbreak My Heart' was presented, David says the group were not very excited. 'It's a chick song,' we said. But they said we could do it as if a guy was singing it. We tried it in English but it just didn't work. We were using too many Toni Braxton-isms, which are great, but just sounded so feminine. The moment we tried doing it in Spanish, the whole flavour turned around a hundred and eighty degrees and everything just clicked,' David told Ritchie Yorke in the South Australian *Sunday Mail.*

This is how Il Divo gives new music a unique opportunity to shine. 'We wanted to bring back classic lyric singing,' says David. 'We've been called "pop opera", but it's more correct to call it "operatic pop". Giorgio Armani supplies our suits, and when we walk down the street, we feel like the pop Mafia. It's very funny.' In the South Australian *Sunday Mail*, journalist Anna Merola discovered a laughing, talkative David finalising these comparisons of Il Divo to the famous informal groups of singers from the 1950s, made up of Frank Sinatra, Sammy Davis Junior and Dean Martin. 'Well, we're not boys, we're all in our thirties and we're a nouveau rat pack – or an operatic rat pack . . . We're a very strong unit. But we try not to be, well, divos about it.'

Still, making that first LP needed a lot of professionalism and planning. There wasn't any time to become friends or to get accustomed to each other's styles in time. The men had to get on with the job. 'We came in and shook hands and said, "OK, we respect each other as artists, now let's make some art." ' David says that Il Divo's kind of music switches between pop and opera, a melding of techniques with flourishes and climaxes that many wouldn't expect. Singing in different languages and trying to decide what language to sing which tune in posed other challenges. 'We tried singing in English, Spanish and Italian and some of the songs have full versions of each, so we ended up recording some forty-five tracks, of which twelve ended up on the album.'

Il Divo has no leader – unless you count Simon Cowell. 'Il Divo is a democracy,' David has said. Without a lead singer – they all share leads from one time to another – they have learned to work in harmony with each other. 'We're pretty stereotypically from our countries. If Carlos weren't a singer, he'd be a bullfighter. Sébastien is sensitive and loves fine food and fine wine. Urs is like a Swiss watch; he always likes to be on time. And I'm American, so I talk a lot. But we're all funny and we're like frat boys. This is the first time I've ever had best friends who are guy friends. In high school, growing up in a conservative state like Colorado, singing was not cool. But it's cool being in Il Divo.' For Simon Cowell, David has nothing but admiration. 'He speaks his mind clearly and concisely; it's black and white for him, so if he doesn't like it, he really doesn't like it, or if he likes it, he absolutely loves it. But he's given us a lot of latitude [with this album], and it's been a collaborative effort.'

When asked about the most romantic thing he's ever done, David recounts the time he was auditioning for Il Divo. 'I was in Paris, and I hadn't seen my girlfriend for quite some time; I actually flew her to Paris. I tell you there's nothing better to me than having a nice romantic dinner, drinking champagne, walk down the Seine river and then . . .' The strain of fame and performing and being away from home and loved ones is not lost on David.

In fact, he stresses that the men of Il Divo are not superhuman or merely mannequins swathed in Armani. 'We are completely normal men, so we often have jeans and T-shirts,' he says. 'If we're wearing smart clothes on stage, we feel pretty good. It is like going on a date. You want to dress up and look good. Like if you are going to dinner with a sexy girl – or a man in Carlos's case . . .' David is unable to resist making fun of Carlos's apparent eye for the ladies. 'Urs likes heavy metal, Sébastien likes pop, and I am crazy for techno,' says David. 'We're just four guys with trained voices doing what we do best! Since we got into the io, the Il Divo sound has just evolved and what we've now created is something completely new and extremely exciting,' says David. The members of Il Divo, and in particular David Miller, are vocal, interesting, normal men – with the exception that they can sing their hearts out, make us cry with their voices and look heart-meltingly beautiful wearing nothing but a towel.

In American interviews, David comes across best, being able to pick up cultural references and other allusions that may be lost on the more inter-national members of the group. During a TV interview with Hammer from ABC FOX TV, Il Divo, accompanied by Simon Cowell, began to talk about their music. Cowell started by saying that the kind of music they are doing will be more popular in the future because 'I think people are beginning to appreciate great voices again. I met these four guys, one from Switzerland, one from Spain, one from France and one from America. We introduced them, and we said this is what we would like to do. We would like to make this music popular all over

'Il Divo has no leader – they all share leads from one time to another – they have learned to work in harmony with each other'

the world. Let's just match fabulous songs with great voices, and these guys have a lot of charisma, and thank God it worked.'

When the host asked the group about giving up their solo careers, David chipped right in. 'Well, I mean for myself, it really was a question of timing. If you had come to me ten years ago while I was still trying to climb up the opera ladder and present this to me, I'm not so sure I would have jumped on it as readily, but it's to the point now we're all in our thirties. I think it's just a question of perfect timing.'

David sees the ultimate appeal of Il Divo's music to be for women who 'might want an extra surge of romance in their lives'.

Then came the inevitable American joke: the fact that Il Divo phonetically sounds like Devo, the group from Ohio that had a song called 'Whip It'. The host couldn't resist jumping in with the question 'I was actually wondering if anybody has suggested you do a remake of the song "Whip It". But it's a really bad joke. Are you the only one who gets that reference?' To this, David admitted, 'I'm the only one who gets that. Potted plants on your head.' (The potted plant reference is one only Devo fans will understand and appreciate.)

Along with his fellow Divos, David knows that his hard work and talent are not squandered in the group. The music that they make, the people they touch, and the limelight that descends upon them is what music is about – emotion, feeling, being transported to another place merely by the sound of the human voice. As for what Il Divo's music actually is, David says the public are still finding a word for it. 'Some people call it pop, some people call it opera. Some people call it crossover, some people call it pop opera, some actually just call it popera, but what we do is, we sing [pop] with operatic classical techniques; we don't actually sing any opera.' And he should know, because he has.

SEBASTIEN IZAMBARD

'The thing is, if you do good music and you're good
at performing it, then it will just happen for you.'
Sébastien Izambard

Sébastien Izambard was born on 7 March 1973 in France. A tenor in pitch,
Sébastien's voice is the 'vox populi' – the pop singer, the popular voice – of the
group. The only member of Il Divo who has had no formal music training,
Sébastien nevertheless brings to Il Divo several necessities. He taught himself
the piano as well as the acoustic guitar while still very young, although at one
stage he considered becoming an airline pilot.

Early in his life, Sébastien found himself performing on the barges around
Paris and it was those experiences that brought home to him the fact that
music was his love – and he worked hard, relying on himself and his own tastes
to make his way in the competitive, cliquey world of pop music. He did what
all self-made musicians have to do: record demos and make many visits to many
different record companies. His first contract was with EMI, a fortunate thing,
which even today Sébastien finds remarkable. 'I had unbelievable luck. To be able

to devote myself entirely to what I love – it's truly a luxury. Getting through takes a long time. You really have to search yourself, musically.'

His tastes are diverse: Radiohead, Jeff Buckley, Jacques Brel, Johnny Hallyday, Queen, Razorlight, Maroon 5, Keane, Scissor Sisters and Coldplay. His native language is French, but he speaks English and a bit of Italian and is learning Spanish. His hobbies, when he has time, are flying, swimming, tennis and he adores Jelly Babies and good red wine. (Food obviously plays a major role in Sébastien's world view. Commenting to a reporter from *The Hindu* newspaper, he quipped, 'Unfortunately we don't really know much about the music scene in India, but I really love Indian food!')

Six foot tall, with green eyes, Sébastien has formed himself into an accomplished songwriter and producer for many French musicians in Paris. The LP entitled *Libre*, Sébastien's first solo album, was released in June 2001. Its release caused him to be dubbed 'the new prodigy of French pop'. His inspiration for the LP was the south-west of France, and he has been described as possessing 'a hot voice . . . luminous like the sand dunes of the Atlantic coast'. Discussing the LP's inspiration, Sébastien said, 'Between Les Charentes, Les Landes and La

Nollane   Bàn Laurent   Nicaud

Thomas Gérôme   Sébastien Izambard

Lorène Devienne   et Julie Wingens

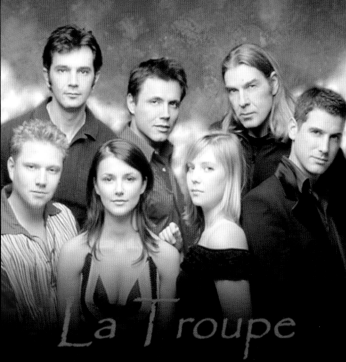

Les plus grands succés des Comédies Musicales, Dessins Animés & Films
sur scène !!

La Troupe

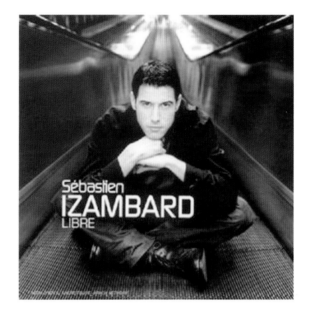

Sébastien
IZAMBARD
LIBRE

'The sheer emotion that singing in an operatic fashion generates to the listener is what inspired us - it's pure, it's classical, and it's deep. There are some operatic pieces that have made our hair stand and at times even made us cry'

Gironde, my family links are very strong. It's where I always spent all my holidays. I love the food, the dunes, the pine trees, the ocean, the surf and the swimming. Hossegor, Capbreton, Le Pyla, Le Ferret, but also Angoulême and the surrounding area.' As a confessional LP and a telling portrait of an artist as a young man, Sébastien put the pull of nature and the sea into the music. 'In front of these horizons, you feel less artifice, less conditioning.'

Penning eleven songs for his debut, Sébastien was given lyrical support by the famous Lionel Florence, who has also supplied lyrics for Johnny Hallyday, French rock pop star Florent Pagny, platinum-selling singer Patricia Kaas and pop idol Pascal Obispo, an innovative (and tattooed) French pop star who had a hit with his debut tune 'Plus Que Tout Au Monde' and who went on to achieve sales of half a million in France alone. Upon the release of *Libre* Sébastien was called 'the new Obispo'. Sébastien was flattered, happy to be an artist compared with anyone who had come before him. 'What matters is to not cheat with my voice and my music. It's all about giving your best to people. To touch them, to tell them a story. To accept being in this skin and suffering for the one thing which really matters – love.' Indeed, Sébastien's songs range between tender, catchy pop tunes and ballads of love, both metaphorical and real.

Sébastien went on to another high point of his solo career: supporting Johnny Hallyday in August 2001 at his Parisian Olympia concert. Hallyday, who kept Izambard as one of his many young musical associations, showed him a little of what fame and legend looks like from the inside. Sébastien says of that time, 'I find he has a voice and an admirable presence. I have a lot of respect for his professionalism. When he gets on the stage, believe me, nobody has their hands in their pockets.' The Hallyday concerts were an edifying experience for the then seasoned musician and singer: 'L'Olympia was magical. Two thousand people every night [were in the audience]. At first, I had stage fright, but as it turned out I was fine, and I gave it everything.' In the following year Sébastien was given a plum role as Le Businessman in Richard Cocciante's musical production of *Le Petit Prince*. The musician was working on his second LP when he joined Il Divo. With his songwriting and production skills, he plans to provide more original material for the group to perform.

During an interview on 31 March 2005 on Perth 720 ABC with Australian radio presenter Eoin Cameron, who was already a fan of the group, Sébastien summed up his Il Divo experience so far, beginning with the idea of Simon Cowell's to unite four classical male voices into one group – following the Andrea Bocelli version of Cowell's initial inspiration. Although he was a seasoned performer and musician, the audition was nevertheless intimidating – even more so when Sébastien saw the competition he was up against and what the aim of the auditions ultimately was. 'I've never sung true opera,' he admitted in one interview. 'At the audition I nearly left when I heard the others' voices, but David [Miller] said I should be myself and it worked.' He also added that the different cultures between the men did cause some problems but that after spending a year together, those problems were now nonexistent. 'We just have to have, you know, [use] eye contact, and we understand each other totally now, so the issues with culture and language, really, it's finished.'

When pressed to talk about the other members of Il Divo, Sébastien only laughs and goes into a by now well-rehearsed litany of acceptable criticism of his fellow singers. 'Well, David is the crazy one, always joking and playing around. Carlos is a volcano, very Spanish, always saying what he thinks. Urs is very quiet. He likes everything on time and neatly tied up.' As for Sébastien himself, he isn't sure how others see him, but the other members of Il Divo always assist by yelling in unison, 'He's French!' Urs, ever articulate and observant, says that Sébastien 'is discreet, but he has strong opinions and is very sensitive. He reacts the most to small things. If we're in a restaurant and his food is too spicy, he'll stand up and tell everyone.'

'People are fed up with the fast-food industry of music. They want something more real. There's a lack of true romance and good voices, artists who sing with heart and passion, and we're filling the gap'

Sébastien's understanding of the recording process was a big help to the group. Two days after meeting for the first time, they were recording their first album with 'Unbreak My Heart' rearranged by the entire group. Everyone in Il Divo was well acquainted with the romantic hit, to the point where they felt they almost couldn't get away from Toni Braxton's version of it, both the original slow version and the later dance remix. Sébastien, speaking as proud producer and pop songwriter, commented of the final result, 'We really made something that didn't exist of that song. We were really proud because I thought we found the balance of the pop and the opera.'

As concerned with the material as he is with performing – and, arguably putting the pop in Il Divo – Sébastien thinks that the melding of classical and pop influences makes the songs unique. 'The songs sound like they're made for us, which is great, as we were all scared by this venture after having successful solo careers.' Being drawn together with a common purpose, Sébastien agrees that, 'People are fed up with the fast-food industry of music. They want something more real. There's a lack of true romance and good voices, artists who sing with heart and passion, and we're filling that gap.'

Sébastien seems to understand Cowell better than anyone else in the group. 'I had heard that Simon had a reputation for being very rude. He's turned out to be the nicest person in the business.' This is not to say that Sébastien, as with the other seasoned members of the group, were pushovers for Cowell's vision

'The effects of a sustained,
fully developed human voice
are almost other wordly'

or ferocious reputation. All members of Il Divo have worked long and hard to get where they are vocally and professionally and that requires more than a little work on personal boundaries. It is one thing to take advice and another to be pushed around and moulded in a way that chafes. On a Finnish website interview, Sébastien once remarked of Cowell that 'If he spoke to us the way he does to those kids on TV, we'd kill him. We're too mad and too old for that. We're not youngsters whom he can manipulate.' And when members of Il Divo comment on other singers, they usually have well-defined ideas about who is a professional and who is not. Without being egotistical or big-headed, Sébastien knows all too well about the competitive nature of singing and the business of music and where his talents fit in. The people who go on shows such as *Pop Idol* and *American Idol* perhaps do not have his insight. Defending Cowell's comments to the amateur performers on those popular TV shows, Sébastien says, 'These people who aren't very good at singing only go along to these shows to get five minutes of fame . . . So I think it's right that he says what he thinks about them.'

Sébastien, like the other members of Il Divo, wasn't clued-up about the non-French TV and radio programmes around the world that the group have given interviews to. The less he knew about the show, the happier he was. 'I have to say, it was quite funny for me. I don't know any of these shows, so you arrive there, you have no pressure, you get there, and you have such fun, a good time there . . . Our lives have totally turned around after the release of the album. We never expected to be this huge, a phenomenon. When we performed on the *Oprah Show*, the audience went crazy.' For Sébastien, and the others, the whole Il Divo phenomenon has been a whirlwind ride and a dream come true. But the cost has been a dislocation of family, career and personal lives. Few of Il Divo get to see their family or friends, living as they do either on the road or in the recording studio.

Still, what keeps Sébastien going is the power of the music and the fact that the group is creating new and beautiful music that is enjoyed by more people than any of its participants thought possible. Sébastien is not an opera singer, or even a classical singer. But he knows the impact that good music has: 'The sheer emotion that singing in an operatic fashion generates to the listener is what inspired us — it's pure, it's classical, and it's deep. There are some operatic pieces that have made our hair stand and at times even made us cry.'

Sébastien has one of the most playful attitudes within Il Divo. Always ready to make a joke or rise to an occasion (or a dare), he's the one who will answer that embarrassing question from a naughty TV or radio host when the other members may not be ready to open their mouths. In several instances, Sébastien has taken on difficult questions with great confidence and style. When asked once, in accordance with the song 'My Way', if he could do it his way, he completed the sentence, 'If I could do it my way, I'd sing it!'

Of course, flirtatious questions always come up with Sébastien. In fact, flirtatious questions are part and parcel of being a member of Il Divo. When asked about the sexiest time he ever had, Sébastien quite unashamedly answered, 'I actually rode in a wagon. That was her birthday. We took the train from Paris to Venice . . . And then we went to Venice and to the best hotel and we made love all night and it was beautiful!'

In accordance with his playful and unabashed nature, Sébastien was once quoted in a British tabloid newspaper as saying that he wouldn't mind comforting Sienna Miller in her time of need. The beautiful actress at the time had just split from her boyfriend, actor Jude Law, and was in some distress. Again, when pressed about 'the art of passion' by a newspaper reporter and asked straight out if he was the adventurous type, Sébastien retorted with 'You mean like Indiana Jones? Yes, I do it with a hat and a whip.' On a German TV programme, Sébastien commented that he was surprised that so many people from so many countries loved Il Divo – to the point where he was going to have to get a map and pins and plot out what he called 'a fairytale'. On the same show, Sébastien cunningly answered a query of 'Are you romantic?' with an equally challenging answer: 'You have to try us and then you have to tell us.'

Sébastien will be penning more tunes for Il Divo, learning more about classical music and voices and bringing the pop into the group's sensational hybrid pop opera sound. He may record some solo material in the future but, as he himself has said, 'For now Il Divo is my priority.'

URS BUHLER

'They were screaming at us. But I'm sure I also heard one ask her mate, "Who are we waving to?" '

Urs Buhler

Fresh-faced and urbane, Urs Buhler, Il Divo's Swiss-born tenor, has almost Keanu Reeves-style good looks matched with a fine tenor voice. He is famous for proving, on a British TV talk show that, of all the members of Il Divo, he can hold a note the longest (forty-three seconds) – a mean feat under camera lights, the watchful eyes of a nation and your fellow singers. Urs's tenor voice is the middle range of Il Divo's multi-harmonic sound, unifying and reed-like, with the ability to flex and punch the melody when needed. With fine features, longer hair than the other members of the team and a wry sense of humour, Urs's take on the whole Il Divo phenomenon is seriously at odds with anyone who thinks fame turns everyone's heads. With Urs Buhler, music wasn't a choice: it was his destiny. Born on 19 July 1971 in Willisau, near Lucerne, Switzerland, the tenor – famous amongst fans for his light-coloured eyes which provoke arguments over whether they qualify as hazel or grey – stands at about five foot ten. He took music seriously from very early on and was performing by his late teens – rock singing, which challenges a voice so young. 'I sang in a boys' choir, and at seventeen I joined a hard rock band.' The band was Conspiracy, based in his home town of Lucerne, and he was the front man. It was clear from then on that singing publicly was an important part of Urs's life, though only part of his musical experience. He attended his town's music school, the Lucerne School of Music. Growing up speaking Swiss German, he also speaks German, Dutch, English and French. Urs plays the piano and, true to a rebellious, risk-taking streak, rides and restores motorcycles.

Urs's love of music was aided by the fact that Lucerne also hosts a globally renowned classical music festival, which in turn spawned the school he first attended. The Lucerne School of Music specialises in classical and jazz, giving Urs an educational insight other singers may lack. Another notable feature of the school is its focus on preparing its students for the business of music with emphasis on a serious career doing what you are trained to do. While the school setting was a far cry from the loud, exciting music he would perform in the evening, its training provided a solid base for what was to come. At a time when almost every teen in town wanted to be a rock musician or singer, Urs took the hard route of studying classical music, at that time not terribly hip. His reason? Inspiration. After hearing a track famously used in the film *Excalibur*, Urs made his choice: 'I decided to study classical music after hearing Carl Orff's "Carmina Burana".'

After his studies at the academy, he moved to Holland where he continued training his exceptional voice at the Amsterdam Conservatory under the watchful eye of Udo Reinemann, a teacher whose masterclasses include the work of Schubert, Strauss, Mahler, Mendelssohn, Schumann, Liszt and Brahms. This serious study of music was followed by even more one-on-one tuition, this

time with private lessons from the famous Swedish tenor and respected opera singer Gösta Winbergh – a performer noted for his good looks and 'golden' tone. Urs also studied with French opera singer Christian Papis, who was known for perfecting his role in Bizet's *Carmen*. With one season at the Salzburg Festival – singing in the choir under the tutelage of legendary conductor Claudio Abbado – Urs's subsequent singing experience was in Holland, most notably with the Netherlands Opera. In fact, Urs is a bit of a star in Holland; singing extensively on that country's oratorio circuit for seven years, he's made a name for himself.

Urs had to think long and hard about abandoning the career he had strived to achieve before even auditioning for Il Divo. When Simon Cowell offered an audition, Urs didn't have a clue what the music Svengali wanted or what Il Divo was all about. Who could have known when the concept was still so new? After careful consideration, Urs took the plunge and had a private audition with Cowell, after which he knew Il Divo was the right choice. The attractions are many, but Urs has said in an interview with *XX*, 'I think that we make more pop music than opera, but it is an opportunity to make something new. In fact, we haven't chosen mere pop songs; we are singers of lyrics and that touches people personally. That makes all the difference.' Urs's opinion holds out. Though Urs and the others were told that the fanbase of Il Divo was only going to be mums, the facts prove that prediction wrong. 'You always hope that things will go the best way possible, obviously, but you can never expect it. So I was very surprised – even more about the reactions to the music, which are very positive in a market that is difficult at the moment. That exceeds my wildest dreams.'

Not that Urs really saw the pop star effect of Il Divo straight away. Being so involved with making music for so many years may have made him immune to the crowds. It will be only a matter of time before the swooning fans, who may not as yet be flinging their undergarments on stage, start getting very personal indeed. 'I didn't really see the effect the music had on people at first,' Urs says, 'but it is true that some of the reactions I saw were distracting . . . Personally, I think that it is the effect of the romantic music and this is the reason I sing. But everyone hears what they want to hear. In any case, when I am recognised in the street, everyone's very polite. I can travel all alone on a bus and not be recognised. It is the group that gets the attention.' That said, getting or giving attention is easy for Urs. Not a rash person, he has bags of hidden confidence, the kind that doesn't need flagging to be noticed. For example, when asked in

'I think that we make more pop music
than opera, but it is an opportunity to
make something new'

an interview what was the most romantic thing he'd ever done, he replied, 'I knew this girl for five weeks. Then I had to leave for Austria, because we sang there for six weeks, so I hadn't seen her. After the last performance, I jumped into the car and drove a hundred and ten kilometres back to Amsterdam. And knocked on her door at nine a.m.' Just in time for breakfast, one thinks. And no, this story had no influence on the video for 'Regresa A Mi' – the girl standing at the train station who, fans have noted, seems to have an uneasy relationship with the boy on her left as she waves Urs goodbye. In *People* magazine, on 27 June 2005, Urs confessed, 'I like dancing, but I am inhibited. I don't let loose that easily. I find dancing very personal and sexual.'

After much soul-searching about whether to join the band, Urs admits, 'I cancelled other engagements after meeting Simon.' As for his relationship with the other men of Il Divo, Urs can only lavish praise, a rare thing in the competitive world of classical singing. 'The other members of Il Divo are fantastic,' he has said, recounting the days of recording the first CD when the entire group was living together in a series of apartments in Chelsea, a part of London of which Urs has fond memories. To ensure that there was no favouritism shown, Urs recalls that they lived in four identical flats in a block, to indicate the equality of each voice. Indeed, Urs agrees that Il Divo is more than the sum of its parts. It is a well-balanced, well-oiled machine where 'every voice has its own strengths'.

Despite his early experience as the lead singer of a rock group, Urs's many years of classical training gave him vocal skills of a different sort. Hence, there were some challenges trying to achieve the now unique sound of Il Divo. Urs said, 'I found it hard to make pop effects, to be quirky or breathy. I told Simon, "I'm a classical singer and that's what I'm going to do," and he accepted it.'

A seasoned professional and used to the ways of the road, Urs found touring quite comfortable. His head isn't turned by the group's success. Unlike the naïve pop idols of old, Urs seems to know that fame's a game, even if the band has brought recognition on a global scale. The excitement around Il Divo? 'It's a big, big, fun roller-coaster ride.' Enjoying the group's popularity and their chart success is easy for the Swiss singer because he knows the great adage of acclaim: enjoy the applause but don't believe it. Their success seems to be almost magical. Who would have thought that pristine classical cover versions of pop hits could take over countries, even without being on a radio playlist?

Urs respects Simon Cowell's acumen when it comes to judging how music relates to its audience. But with all the training and time Urs has put into honing his craft, sharpening his skills, it makes sense for him as an artist to find the ultimate platform upon which to display his talent. For example, when Urs and the others wanted to sing 'My Way', and help arrange the song as well, there was little opposition from those who were supposed to be forming the sound of the group. Unlike the rush to record that first album so soon after they'd met, 'For the second album, which we record in July and August, we have more time for preparation and we're gathering ideas according to our tastes.'

Cowell's packaging of stars was well known to some, particularly those in the UK where his singing creations are usually launched. Urs admits that he wasn't very aware of Simon Cowell in any of his guises, including his role as the *American Idol* judge. Urs admits that 'I had never heard of that person before. So I had no idea of what he was doing, no idea about his reputation as "Mr Nasty" . . . So I was totally blank. I only knew it was an audition for some cross-over project. That's everything I knew.' As it turns out, the fearsome Simon Cowell made the best impression on the young tenor, who has said that Cowell is 'a very clever guy, very charming and very honest . . . great – actually very nice'. So it seems that if you have talent, are trained and take yourself and your art seriously before you meet Cowell, he'll respect you and – in Urs Buhler's case – give you a job.

Urs is down-to-earth and serious about his craft. And yet his feelings about Il Divo's 'packaging' are not in conflict with his more artistic ideals. He casually says that the way Il Divo came together was no different from the casting of any opera – one goes through one's agent, there are auditions and discussions, etc. Of course, Urs sees his voice, and that of the other members of Il Divo, as the primary attraction of the group. But he isn't unaware that looks certainly help to sell songs in the entertainment industry. 'There is absolutely no act in the pop business where the look is not important, even if it is to be ugly. But it always has to fit together, and you know our look and the way we are dressed now, that we are dressed and sponsored by Armani, these things developed once we had the record. Then we got in touch with stylists and we tried out loads of different looks. We had test photo shoots, what looks good, what matches the sound we created on that record. This is just the result of it. Everyone involved with Il Divo thought this works best together.'

Facing critics doesn't bother Urs, even when the finger is pointed at the marketing of the group – for example, their public appearances tend to be very high profile: this isn't a band that stoops to opening supermarkets. They may have as their first American TV appearance the extremely popular *Oprah Winfrey Show*, but Urs does not feel he has made a bad choice. 'In the beginning, people did not know how to take us and the phrase "boy band" appeared rather often. But as soon as people saw us, they realised that that didn't fit. We're all about thirty, we're not kids any more . . . We are, in truth, musicians and singers. We have to find a new term for the perfect mix between classical voice technique and pop – if you want to call it popera, that's fine. It is something new, something that didn't exist before. There's one thing you can't manufacture and that's our voices. And that's just real.'

After his many hard years of training, and with all the time and effort that Il Divo is consuming, Urs is tireless in his pursuit of making classical music available and known to the world – perhaps much in the same way it was before pop, jazz, music hall, blues and rock came along. For Urs, classical music – and that includes classical singing, opera and all forms of lyrical singing – is a world treasure. It should be enjoyed by everyone and well known to all. To sing how he sings is not merely a natural gift. That gift must be honed over years with hours of toil and devotion. The end result is music that sounds like no other, which travels straight to the soul. To leave that kind of music to only a few

'I like dancing, but I am inhibited. I don't let loose that easily. I find dancing very personal and sexual'

people is a waste of a fine experience. As Urs sees it, 'I find it a shame that the classical world is so snobbish. There's something for everyone, but they act like classical is strictly for an elite.'

All of the members of Il Divo are, in the words of one music producer who spied them in an adjacent studio, 'very presentable', but Urs's almost androgynous good looks seem to attract intense attention. For example, one fan drew up his astrological chart, with insights such as 'tends to be moody' and 'values his family and loved ones above all else'. If the stars are right, Urs's moon in Gemini would give him a quick wit and a mind to match. In interview after interview, he has shown that he can think on his feet and he is no one's pushover. In one German TV interview, he resisted the hostess's query about his love life. When he resisted, she insisted, 'No, I am asking you!' Despite her protestations and the ticking clock of the on-air time, Urs wouldn't budge. He apologised and gestured that she should ask someone else. (She ended up turning to Carlos who, in the hostess's words, 'became diplomatic'.) Under that smooth Swiss exterior beats the heart of a more daring, more determined individual whose musical likes include Black Sabbath, Nightwish, Van Halen, Dokken, Eighties and Nineties hard rock and heavy metal.

Although Urs is relaxed about fame, it seems to have played havoc with his personal life. As if trying to handle what was ostensibly a new and important job wasn't strain enough, Urs was also concerned about his girlfriend in France. 'I hardly ever see her,' he said. 'I hope she still knows me when I get back.' The dedication to Il Divo means that any family member or loved one won't be seen

'Every voice has its own strengths'

for weeks or months at a time. This goes for every single one of the group members: all are sacrificing any established relationships they had before they ever heard of Simon Cowell. And the added female attention from the armies of fans won't make their girlfriends back home very happy either. But, with an opportunity like this, Urs knows that he must make sacrifices. 'A chance like this to do such a high-profile project, let me call it, the way you can start already on such a level, like launching the CD and all these TV shows in the States and everything, that is just a once-in-a-lifetime chance. If you don't grab it, that's not coming along again.' Luckily, he, like Carlos Marín, likes the travelling aspect: 'Being in Montreal yesterday with, I don't know, zero degrees, and being in Miami today lying in the sun, that's fabulous.'

Urs is no one's fool. Fame gives those who have it an advantage, a platform for talent that wouldn't otherwise be on offer. 'I like music for the cause of making the music, for the cause of singing and for the cause of bringing something to the audience, making them feel good. You can take your message along to a lot of people around the world.'

CARLOS MARIN

'But we are clever guys, and we have a lot of tricks. For example, if you miss a note, make sure you are smiling.' Carlos Marin

Arguably the most traditionally masculine of the four, Carlos Marin – who often calls himself 'Carlitos' on the Il Divo website message boards – is the only baritone within the group. In musical terms, this means his voice is lower than that of David, Sébastien and Urs but is between the lowest male voice in opera, the bass, and the higher tenor. His voice, however, is not the deep baritone often associated with evil characters in opera; Carlos's voice is called, within opera circles, a 'Verdi baritone', which means he can access the higher tones of his range with ease while, if he so chooses, slink down to the lower range as well. A Verdi baritone has much more flexibility in what he can sing with ease than other baritones, and this is one reason why Il Divo couldn't survive without him. He's the sonic backbone, the foundation of the sound, the most distinctive voice of the four. His deep, flexible, rich mahogany tones can be picked out within the breathier moments of 'Regresa A Mi'; in essence, any heavier tone within the group's repertoire will belong to Carlos.

As with The Beatles or The Stones, every fan will have his or her favourite performer. Carlos, however, could be considered the most outwardly seductive-looking of the four divos. With chiselled features, curly black hair, a hairy chest (frequently brandished with an open shirt) and distinctive ears, Carlos is often laughingly referred to — often by himself — as the Latin lover of the group. But his Mediterranean good looks aside, Carlos is not a musical lightweight or someone who went into the music business by default.

Carlos was born in Germany on 13 October 1969, of Spanish parents and spent several years of his life there before moving to Amsterdam and then to Spain, taking masterclasses with Alfredo Kraus, Montserrat Caballé (who so famously sang with the late Freddie Mercury) and Jaime Aragall. Carlos has been a noted singer in many operatic productions. His performances in the Spanish productions of *Les Miserables* were well received amongst critics and public alike, as were his roles in large-scale operas such as *La Traviata*, *The Marriage of Figaro*, *The Barber of Seville*, *La Bohème* and *Madame Butterfly*. All of these test a performer's ability not only to sing perfectly, but also to act, hit marks and cues, and interact convincingly with other performers while wearing heavy make-up and costume. Clearly, opera isn't easy. But for Carlos, so in demand on the opera stage that the offers of roles far outstripped his availability, the performance is key. No wonder then that when asked, Carlos has said that his favourite pop music singers include Tom Jones, Elvis Presley and Freddie Mercury. Every single one of those performers — and Queen as a group along with frontman Freddie Mercury — were known as ground-breaking singers and musicians who gave spectacular performances. The same extends to Carlos within Il Divo: he loves to perform — a fact that surfaces whenever he appears on stage or near a camera.

While some professionals find that they cannot spare the energy for humour while they work, Carlos seems to be just the opposite. His apparently boundless energy extends to a playful sense of fun, which comes to the fore in virtually every interview. Most of all, Carlos likes to play up to his sexy image as the man every woman wants. (He once replied, when asked if he could do something his way, that he would give his phone number to every woman.) He doesn't try to put a damper on his sassy, saucy ways. In *People* magazine, on 27 June 2005, Carlos quipped, 'I like smaller women. It is easier to walk with them, hold their hands in the street, hug them.' Adding up all of Carlos's comments

'I love to sing love songs,
I'm a very romantic guy, but I'm
not a player. You must have love in life'

on the fairer sex can lead to some interesting conclusions. For example, the 'small women' don't even have to be real women: Carlos once joked that the most romantic thing he ever did was going to Disneyland, booking the best suite in the hotel and then showing up with Mickey Mouse's girlfriend, Minnie. In an interview for the Toronto *Sun*, journalist Valerie Gibson asked Carlos his thoughts about groupies – and in particular older women who may find Il Divo completely irresistible. 'Now that would be interesting, and exciting,' Carlos joked to her. Clearly, he relishes playing the hot-blooded Spanish baritone to the cooler French and Swiss singers and the strait-laced American tenor.

In reality, Carlos doesn't take the idea of being the seductive Spanish singer with the massive voice very seriously. In an interview with journalist Lara Ceroni for Canadian *Elle* magazine, he said, 'Everyone feels connected to romantic music; everyone can relate to it. What can I say? I'm Spanish, a Latino lover! I love to sing love songs, I'm a very romantic guy, but I'm not a . . . what do you call it? A player? You must have love in life.' Although Carlos further flirted with the journalist by laughing and answering the question of what inspires him with 'looking at you', he finished his laughing and got down to properly addressing the question of his involvement in music. His began earlier than any of the other members of the group – being a musical prodigy at the age of eight, and putting his first record out two years later, at the age of ten. In this way, Carlos has grown up in the music industry; it is his life, whether his involvement has been operatic or singing leads in *Les Miserables*, *Man of La Mancha* or *La Traviata* as well as *Beauty and the Beast*, *Peter Pan* and several other Spanish musicals. Carlos takes his experience, his caramel baritone voice and his reputation into the mix of Il Divo partly because of his love of experimentation – as well as knowing that he has done virtually everything else offered in the music industry. If it is musical, chances are that Carlos will thoroughly enjoy it.

Fans may notice his eyes – which they like to describe as honey-brown – and comment that he is probably the shortest member of Il Divo, at about five foot ten, but that doesn't matter. Carlos's Cuties, as they are called, are fans of the baritone wherever he goes. He may have quipped in an interview on German TV that he likes to have a woman in every port, but Carlos could conceivably pull that fantasy off as he speaks Spanish as his native tongue, with a great command of English and German, and a bit of Italian thrown in for good measure.

In an interview with Peter Holmes of Australia's *Sunday Telegraph*, on 8 May 2005, Carlos said that his career was so exceptional that he was getting warnings from other professionals about leaving it for Il Divo. In fact, a director said to him that he must be crazy to even consider joining three other soloists in a group. Carlos's excuse was, 'But I wanted to grow as a singer, and what we do does not hurt opera.' And, of course, after Il Divo's first album came out, Carlos went back to Spain and played the music to the man who had initially told him that he was insane to even think about abandoning his career; he promptly admitted that the music was brilliant. In fact, the success of Il Divo means that Carlos has, up to this point, cancelled all of his singing engagements until 2008 merely to focus on the group's progress.

Il Divo's music borrows from many pop and classical sources – 'Nella Fantasia' is taken from the haunting theme of the seminal 1980s film *The Mission*, soundtracked by Ennio Morricone – but the uniting theme is love. Whether Il Divo are singing about motherly love, romantic love, true love or eternal love, the voices and the arrangements reflect the lasting nature of these universal qualities, showing that the greatest opera songs and the greatest pop songs are often built around the same great notions. Carlos has his own theory about the music's appeal: 'I think the people have begun to like us because they were bored with always listening to the same kind of music.'

In an interview with Shuhaidah Saharani in the Malay *Mail* in August 2005, Carlos says, 'I remember when we started to make the Il Divo album, we didn't know how to find the Il Divo sound. So we were trying to figure out which kind of voice, which kind of song . . . so we make it old style. Like the beginning of the song, it was done very soft and in a very pop way, and then we finished the song in the most operatic way that we can. So it's a mix of everything – opera style, musical theatre style, pop style. But we begin the song in a very whispered, soft way.'

On the first album, Carlos admits that his favourite song is 'Regresa A Mi', the video of which at the time of its release was shown in almost constant rotation on global TV. Kidding Carlos about the video, Peter Holmes asked if Carlos really did leave his wife and child in order to join Il Divo. Did the Spaniard leave a young wife in a bad neighbourhood, dooming her to a life trapped in a tiny flat with a baby and letting her see the father of her child only on TV? Could he be that cruel? Carlos laughed and said, 'No. I don't have a baby and a wife at the moment. The script of the videoclip was written by the director Sharon Maguire, who was also the director of *Bridget Jones's Diary*. It was an amazing video but it has nothing to do with our real lives.'

One does wonder, however, why Carlos is the only one in the video who seems to be slinking off to a new city, leaving a wife – or girlfriend – literally holding the baby. The other members of Il Divo are merely trying to find a new way of life, escaping small towns, dead-end jobs and doing an honest day's work. Meanwhile, the suave, powerfully voiced and confident Carlos is seen dodging scooters, sidestepping potentially troublesome thugs in the narrow streets and not even blowing a kiss to the woman who, it seems, has borne his child. Either this is a small joke at the Spaniard's flirtatious ways or a saucy gesture at his Latin lover tag.

Whatever the video suggested, when Lara Ceroni interviewed Carlos Marin, she was treated to a blast of his charm from the start. The baritone told her she was sexy – something any Il Divo fan would long to hear. Then, as is his habit, he settled down to the serious matter at hand: the story of how he became the glossy, dark part of Il Divo. According to Carlos, he was singing in a Dublin opera when he heard the news about the Cowell auditions. 'My manager approached me about sending my videotape to a record label, Sony BMG, as they were potentially scouting out solo singers. I had no idea that I would be auditioning for a group.' After the audition went well, he was asked if he wanted to become part of a quartet; the answer was, for a soloist of his calibre, a resounding no. Carlos considers himself, now and then, an opera singer not terribly interested in pop or any other singing. But several days passed and Simon Cowell himself contacted Carlos and requested a personal meeting. Like the other members of Il Divo, Carlos didn't know Simon Cowell's reputation or career. And so he tells the story that Simon Cowell was inspired by watching a concert of The Three Tenors – José Carreras, Plácido Domingo and Luciano Pavarotti – before he came up with the idea of the operatic supergroup of which Carlos was to become a member. The musical creator had to think about how best to use formally trained voices in a mix of traditional, classical music with pop tunes, both original and cover songs.

Carlos admits to Ceroni that he wasn't sold on Cowell's great pop opera concept immediately. 'He didn't convince me right away,' said Carlos. 'I was doing opera and, before that, musical theatre. It's very difficult to move from this to pop music. My opera directors kept telling me, "Carlos, you're crazy, you're going to ruin your opera career." But I went for it anyhow. It was a very big risk at the time as I didn't know where this would take me.' As it turned out, Simon Cowell

'Everyone feels connected to romantic music; everyone can relate to it'

was a very good judge of vocal quality as well as appearance – and how the group would mesh in the ear and on the eye. Despite his caustic reputation, there is wisdom in his words. And some diplomacy too, having to deal with seasoned professionals such as the men in Il Divo – mostly Carlos, who, in comparison to the other members, has chalked up more musical miles. At this point in the story, Carlos finds Simon Cowell's input an indispensable, guiding light. In one interview on American TV, Carlos quipped that Cowell thinks of Il Divo as his creation, his child almost. 'Yeah, he said always that he's very proud of us, and we're like his little kids, so he's like our dad. Well, he was the inventor of this project so, yeah, yeah, we're very proud of it,' to which the host responded that the group must call him Dad. Carlos was very quick to counter that idea. No, none of the group would *ever* refer to Cowell as 'Dad'.

The bet was a good one. Although Carlos may have, for the time being, given up his hard-earned and high-profile opera career, the fact that Il Divo is a bestselling, ground-breaking opera group is reward enough for taking such a risk. Carlos thinks that their popularity isn't much to do with looks or marketing. According to the baritone, 'We bring something different to the table, I think. We have a very unique sound. Classical arias are mixed with popular, catchy music, and there really isn't anything quite like it out there right now.'

Pop music is generally sung in English, or at least American English – something that could have caused problems for the Il Divo catalogue. But Il Divo is not pitched solely at the pop market or the American sector. One element of Il Divo's amazing, widespread lovability is that the group is multi-lingual and that their songs reflect that. Even a seasoned professional such as Carlos was surprised by their success. He recounts how the finished album made all of them apprehensive. What if the Il Divo bet didn't come off? What if all of them had given up their personal lives, solo careers and future plans for something that no one was going to understand or enjoy? Carlos admits that the group would have been happy if the album had sold 100,000 units – that would have been considered successful in the world of classical music and operatic singing. But when the CD went to the top of the charts in the UK after the first week of its release, the record company affirmed the group's status with another bit of news: the group had in fact replaced Robbie Williams, one of Britain's most popular stars, at number one. The entire group – even the seasoned, unflappable Carlos – was in a state of happy shock.

'Regresa A Mi' was the perfect song to spearhead Il Divo into the public consciousness. In the *Elle* interview, Carlos said that it is a song that 'brought us closer as a group. Simon decided that we should do an operatic spin on this song and we recorded and re-recorded the track fives times in total to see how we could combine all of our harmonies together for one smooth sound.' After putting all of their individual performances in separately, the final result was better than they could have imagined. In a way, 'Regresa A Mi' is the template for the Il Divo singles of the future. After all, as the baritone says, 'There's a thin line between Bono and Freddie Mercury and the great classics.'

According to Carlos, the first album has a sense of urgency about it. The tracks had been more or less predetermined, but there was in the end some flexibility: even if Simon Cowell had had an idea of what tracks should be incorporated, the members of the group did have some say. Carlos says that the addition of Frank Sinatra's big trademark hit 'My Way' was a decision taken by all four of the singers through a bit of a happy accident. One day, during a casual rehearsal, the four suddenly combusted into the song and ended up really enjoying the sound of it. So, no sooner had they decided they liked it, the entire group went into Simon Cowell's office and sang it right in front of him, *a cappella*. Even Simon Cowell, Mr Judgement himself, couldn't resist his four hand-picked singers truly romping through the swanky, swinging classic and so the tune made it on to the album. The second album, *Ancora*, contains more original material and a bit of creativity with guitar and voice work to create some truly terrific, romantic and moving lyrics – something Carlos seems to be very eager to sing.

According to Carlos, 'Il Divo' means 'divine performer'. In the opera world, it is not uncommon for the audience to cry out, 'La Diva! La Diva!' to herald the female singer and praise her voice. Simon, with a keen interest in keeping the group firmly in a more cultural arena, decided upon the name, even if it does mean a single male singer rather than four. Cowell wanted the name to remind people of the opera, of the elegant world of skilled singers, of great emotion and of tremendous excitement – all things that Il Divo is. 'Divo' also suggests, according to Carlos, the sense that a singer can achieve the impossible, that a 'divo' can sing in ways that are otherworldly or superhuman. In an interview in the Malay *Mail*, Carlos was asked whether he considered himself such a divine performer, to which Carlos replied, 'Yes! . . . Nah, I'm just kidding. Of course not.'

> 'Opera used to be regarded like pop music is now, back in the day. I see no reason why it shouldn't be again'

Carlos points out that Il Divo shouldn't really be called a boy band as they sound more mature and are much older than the teens who have made up previous genuine boy bands. What Carlos finds most rewarding about being in the supergroup is sharing the stage with the three other skilled performers: 'Although we're just four normal guys, opera singers,' he told Peter Holmes, 'noble guys if I say so myself, we're maybe in the divine way of being the best of the best but we never look at ourselves as gods or anything divine in that sort of way.' He also says that being surrounded by a huge orchestra in front of 10,000 people in enormous, packed venues is a feeling hard to find elsewhere.

Considering the crowds – and the way that the Il Divo CDs are selling without the aid of usual airplay – it seems the new hybrid of pop and opera, of lyrical classical singing combined with sweeping orchestration and arrangements that emphasise emotion could establish a new genre of popular music. In an interview with the Chicago *Sun-Times* journalist Laura Emerick, Carlos commented, 'Opera used to be regarded like pop music is now, back in the day. I see no reason why it shouldn't be again.'

At work on the second album, *Ancora*, Carlos was hopeful that it would meet its November 2005 deadline, eager to get out of the studio and back into the world. Carlos loves travelling; he adores all the airports, limousines, hotels and taxis that are involved in the life of a performing singer. He says he loves being, in one way or another 'homeless'. If the world tour goes on as planned in 2006, Carlos will be a happy man. He loves the stage, and is energised by performing, revels in the adulation, the singing and the high of using his deep tones to best effect. It is no accident that Carlos Marin has earned the moniker of 'primo baritono'.

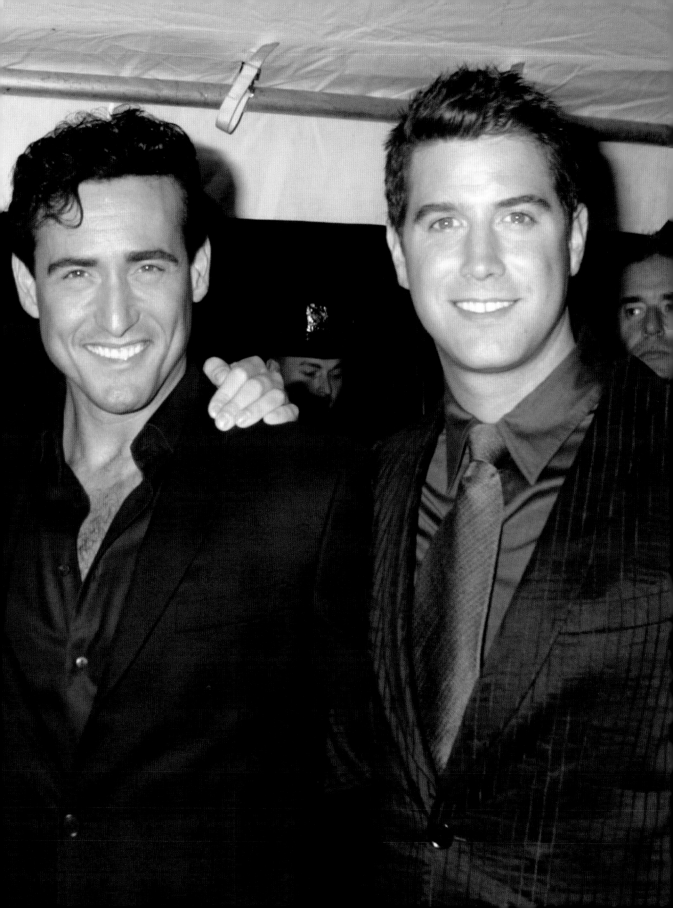

'Il Divo is more than
the sum of its parts.
It is a well-balanced,
well-oiled machine
where every voice
has its own strengths'

IL DIVO

The Music

IL DIVO
THE ALBUM

'Simon brought us together and he deserves all the credit for coming up with the idea, but we have a lot of experience and knowledge about music. If this works, it will be because we have put ourselves into it.'
Urs Buhler

Putting together a band like Il Divo takes time and patience and, as Simon Cowell knows only too well, the input of some very talented people. He has worked with the very best musical talent down the years – composers, producers and writers whose songs have consistently reached the number one spot – and once he had found his perfect singers, it was now time to find the perfect songs for them.

Having been chosen separately from across the globe throughout 2003, they all moved to London in December to meet for the first time, two days before beginning to record the album. 'The boys will tell you it's very common in opera to put people together who don't even know each other,' explains Sébastien. It was imperative the boys did get to know each other, and get along with each other, for they were to be in studios, both in London and in Stockholm, for the next four months. Getting four men, already well-established in their own individual careers, to work together as one smooth unit without clashing egos may have seemed like a tall order, but the mix proved highly successful. For a start, Urs, David, Carlos and Sébastien were all in their thirties and had a level of maturity that ensured there would be no bratty hissy fits. 'We get along really well and leave our egos at the door,' says David.

This mature attitude was to stand them in good stead because it meant they could quickly settle down and work out which sections of particular songs best suited their vocal talents. Carlos says, 'I remember when we started to make the first Il Divo album, we didn't know how to find the right sound. I'm the baritone of the band so my voice is a little darker and deeper. David brings in the typical tenor voice while Sébastien brings in the pop style. Urs brings in this beautiful middle voice from the opera. So, we mix it all together like in a cocktail – that's the magic.'

In order to create magic you need a few spells, or in Il Divo's case a few gorgeously romantic songs, with which to enchant your public. While the boys were getting acquainted, Simon Cowell had already done much of the meticulous groundwork that was to make their debut album such a smash. As David says, 'It was his idea. He went on the search to find the four of us. He said, here are the songs, you guys are the musicians, make me proud.' Finding the perfect songs to get the Il Divo treatment is a much easier task if you have access to the network of talent Simon does. He had chosen the best singers, and now he wanted only the best material for his boys. So he went to people he had already successfully worked with – and you don't get much more successful than songwriters Per Magnusson, David Kreuger and Jorgen Elofsson.

Magnusson and Kreuger had been working for Swedish bands for years but got their big break in 1998 when they started writing for a shy, sixteen-year-old American singer. Her name was Britney Spears. Elofsson, who had become acquainted with the pair back in 1995, started collaborating with them and also worked on Spears's 'You Drive Me Crazy'. The following year all three started writing for Westlife and they contributed to no fewer than four songs on the album *World of Our Own* (including 'Evergreen', which went on to become the fastest-selling single in the history of the UK when it was released by Will Young).

Simon Cowell had signed Westlife to BMG Entertainment International in the UK and Ireland and executive-produced *World of Our Own* and this is how he became acquainted with the songwriters. Now he asked them to write some songs for Il Divo, and they came up with the goods. Magnusson and Kreuger wrote 'Ti Amero' (with Matteo Saggese and Frank Musker), arranged 'Nella Fantasia' and produced 'Every Time I Look At You' and 'Dentro Un Altro Si'. Meanwhile, Elofsson wrote 'Feelings' and co-wrote and produced 'Hoy Que Ya No Estas Aqui'. Working with the famously blunt Cowell obviously didn't put them off, as Elofsson explained in an interview with *Songwriter Universe* magazine, 'Why shouldn't he say what he thinks? I can play Simon a song and he says in his way, "Honestly, Jorgen, that's not your best work." Then it's back to the old drawing board. He's quite a character. You need people like him – a guy who creates record sales. In our hearts we crave music and Simon has a sense of what will work.'

'...nothing is manufactured; we give all the best of our experiences, of our hard work'

The Westlife connection doesn't end there either, for legendary producer Steve Mac (Ronan Keating, Gareth Gates, Samantha Mumba, Atomic Kitten) is a long-term collaborator with the group and on Il Divo he appears as a writer ('The Man You Love'), a producer, arranger and keyboard player. In fact, many of the same studios were used for the recording of Il Divo's and Westlife's music. For the full sixty-piece orchestra on Westlife's 2004 album *Allow Us To Be Frank*, Mac used Phoenix Studios in Wembley, London, where the orchestra on 'Regresa A Mi' was recorded. The other main studio used in London was Rockstone – Mac works for Rockstone Productions. He used a lot of studios in Sweden when he worked on *World of Our Own* and obviously liked the experience because Il Divo used many of the same studios when they flew to Sweden, where tracks with the Stockholm Session Strings were recorded. These included the Sveriges (Swedish) Radio studios and Mono Studio on the island of Skeppsholmen in central Stockholm, owned by a certain Benny Andersson, better known as the bearded one from Abba!

Another songwriter Simon brought onboard was Andy Hill. Andy, with his wife, Nichola, had created the band Bucks Fizz, and Andy had written their winning entry to the Eurovision Song Contest, 'Making Your Mind Up'. Simon knew the couple, and one evening after dinner at their beautiful manor house

'People are beginning to appreciate great voices again'

in West Sussex, complete with its own vineyard (and possibly after a bottle of their award-winning Nyetimber champagne), Simon asked Andy to write some songs for Il Divo. Andy came up with the two tracks produced by Magnusson and Kreuger, 'Every Time I Look At You' and 'Dentro Un Altro Si'.

The decision to use original material that was not necessarily from the operatic canon was a very deliberate one because Simon and the band were keen not to alienate classical music lovers. Simon argues, 'People are so highbrow about classical music. It's a style run by snobs. But I thought, "This could be made more accessible to the public." '

This is why he chose the tracks he did – songs with lush orchestral arrangements and a romantic sweep that could cross over between the classical and pop worlds. Along with the original numbers on the album were three tracks that sounded familiar to many ears but which had been given that special Il Divo twist. The most important of these would turn out to be the world-conquering single, 'Regresa A Mi'. As Toni Braxton's 'Unbreak My Heart', it had reached number two in the UK singles chart in 1996. Now Simon wanted the boys to sing it. They struggled with the song and its phrasing, which seemed unnatural to the boys' opera-trained voices, but all the problems were solved as soon as they tried singing it in Spanish. They had come up with a completely new kind of music. 'Nobody had ever done this type of singing before,' says David, of the technique where all four members share lead vocals through the song and then combine their voices on the soaring choruses and operatic finales.

Another familiar track was 'Nella Fantasia', from *The Mission*. Now with Italian lyrics by Chiara Ferrau, it became a showstopper. However, the most surprising of all the tracks on the album is its last: the boys' very own take on a classic song that had already found fame in the two very different versions of it sung by

Frank Sinatra and Sid Vicious. 'My Way' (or 'A Mi Manera') is a karaoke favourite, a huge great kiss-off of a song to get the emotions stirring. The boys were very aware that including such a famous song could backfire on them. As Sébastien says: 'It's a big challenge because you know that everybody's going to know that song, and they're going to say, "Why are you covering a song that everybody did?" But we did it our way, in the sense that nobody [before] did it or dared to do it in a pop and an operatic way.' It was a gamble that certainly paid off as fans love their version. It also shows that Simon is willing to listen to others' ideas, and that has earned him the respect and admiration of Il Divo. Urs says, 'He's great – actually very nice and he gives good constructive criticism.'

At the end of the studio sessions the band had recorded some forty-five tracks, but it was only the twelve that were considered the *crème de la crème* that ended up on the finished debut album. With the decision made that 'Regresa A Mi' was to be the all-important first single it was time to film the band's debut video. So the boys headed off to Ljubljana in Slovenia for five days to make the mini period drama. The video featured all four members of the band as different characters in their workday clothes. At various locations around the picturesque city (the train station, in a steel works, at the harbour) Urs was seen waving goodbye to his fictional family, David was a steel worker complete with hard hat, while Sébastien played a fisherman and Carlos had a wife and child. As the music swelled the four, in parallel with what had happened in reality, were pictured leaving the people and places they had always known to enter their new existence – within the plush and glamorous confines of a musical theatre, where they would give a performance so rousing it would bring the whole audience to its feet. This was the band Il Divo embracing its destiny – a musical giant performing for the whole world.

Finally, it was time to launch Il Divo on an unsuspecting world, and the response from the public, the real music fans, was phenomenal. Although Sébastien says he understands why some people in the industry would think of the group as manufactured, they are rather missing the point of what Il Divo is all about. 'We're opera singers and we're singing pop songs. This is something nobody has done so far. We wanted to bring opera music to the masses; hence we fused the two musical styles together. I have to say that if you listen to the CD, you can notice that nothing is manufactured; we give all the best of our experiences, of our hard work.'

ON TOP OF
THE WORLD

'You're the guys who knocked me off number one!'
Robbie Williams

Just think what the pressure must have been like: after the search for the four most perfect voices from across the globe, rehearsing and tweaking, recording and re-recording in the studio, it was time for Il Divo to face the world. But was the world ready for them?

The pressure didn't even give Simon Cowell pause for thought; he *knew* they were ready and he had devised a strategy to make sure Il Divo received the best media coverage. After twenty-five years in the business he really should know how. Rather than dilute their impact by spreading the band across every available programme, Cowell adopted the 'less is more' approach and targeted shows he knew would secure the TV audiences most likely to appreciate Il Divo's talents. And the biggest and best of those was good old 'Parky'.

Michael Parkinson is an institution in Britain, so much so that when the celebrity interviewer decided to come out of retirement after many years and resurrect *Parkinson* on TV, his audience switched back on to him in their millions.

This proved invaluable for established artists who wanted to appear on a programme with clout, and for up-and-coming young performers eager to make an impression. One such was a young crossover jazz vocalist and pianist called Jamie Cullum. Jamie didn't even have a recording deal when he sang on Parkinson's Saturday night TV show in 2003, but his appearance sparked a bidding war between music companies and he eventually went on to sign a million-pound deal with Universal.

What was good enough for Jamie Cullum proved even better for Il Divo. Although they had appeared at a hush-hush industry dinner at the end of August 2004, the public had to wait until Saturday 18 September to see them perform on *Parkinson*. The main guests that night were four-time Olympic gold medallist Matthew Pinsent and comedians Lenny Henry and Frank Skinner. The musical slots were filled by no less than REM singing their new single 'Leaving New York' and Il Divo showcasing their first single 'Unbreak My Heart'. With an estimated TV audience of up to 6 million viewers, this was bound to bring the group to the public's notice. But whatever Simon Cowell had been expecting the boys' performance to achieve, even he couldn't have predicted this: three hours after the show, and with a month and a half still to go before its official release, *Il Divo* the album crashed into the number two slot in the pre-release charts.

People who had never even heard of the band before this became diehard fans overnight, and when the album was actually released on 1 November, *Il Divo* rushed straight to the top slot, demoting Robbie Williams's *Greatest Hits*. In fact, at the UK premiere of the movie *Bridget Jones: The Edge of Reason*, Il Divo stumbled into Robbie while on the red carpet. Far from being put out by the encounter, one-time Take That member Robbie said, 'You're the guys who knocked me off number one!' before proceeding to tell them how much he liked their music. If that wasn't endorsement enough, Il Divo was also the first band in twenty-five years to hit the number one album slot without previously having single success. The last band to do that was Led Zeppelin.

From here, Cowell's plan to bring Il Divo to an even bigger audience started to gain momentum, with the band making a succession of exclusive appearances hand-picked to bring the group to the most attentive audiences. On 15 November, the day London submitted its plans to host the 2012 Olympics, Il Divo sang live at the switching-on of the Oxford Street Christmas lights. On a stage erected outside Selfridges the band joined a very starry line up. London's mayor

Ken Livingstone was there, alongside Olympic medallist Sir Steve Redgrave as well as Britain's gold medal-winning relay team and Emma Watson, who plays Hermione in the Harry Potter movies. Many of the 10,000-strong crowd had come to see II Divo, who not only sang 'Unbreak My Heart' but also the traditional carol 'O Holy Night', converting scores more fans with their fabulous music and charming the pants off them by staying to sign autographs afterwards.

II Divo, along with Simon Cowell, were also more than happy to be involved with the BBC's Children In Need appeal. Friday 19 November 2004 marked the twenty-fifth edition of this seven-hour marathon, and by the following morning a staggering £17 million had already been raised.

If November was a memorable month, then December was even more so, as the album remained in the UK top five. It also proved to be hectic, with appearances all over the place. First up on 4 December the boys joined Lionel Richie to provide the live entertainment strands at the fifty-fourth annual Miss World competition, held in China. Beamed direct from the tropical island paradise of Sanya to more than 160 countries, with a combined audience of 2.3 billion, this was by far the biggest media event II Divo had been associated with so far.

By the end of the year *II Divo* had become the tenth biggest-selling album in the UK, while also going multi-platinum in Ireland. There were still areas of the world where it hadn't yet been released: in January 2005 Norway and South Africa finally saw the album's arrival (it subsequently went multi-platinum in Norway as well). But before jetting off to conquer new regions abroad, the boys had a surprise up their collective Armani sleeve. Some very lucky souls got to see them play live at a special sell-out, invitation-only, Mother's Day show at the New Players Theatre, Villiers Street in London on 6 March. Shortly afterwards the album was released in Australia and New Zealand and a whole new continent caught II Divo fever.

What had worked for them in England was to prove just as effective in America. Simon Cowell and his company Syco had agreed with music company Sony BMG that they would target only key American TV slots, and keys don't come much bigger than the *Oprah Winfrey Show*. *Oprah* is broadcast in 117 countries including, bizarrely, Afghanistan, Bahrain, Botswana, Croatia, Iceland, Iran, the Philippines, Qatar, Rwanda and even Uganda.

As Simon Cowell was already known in the States for his appearances on *American Idol*, which has an audience of around 30 million, it made sense for him

'I don't know what they were singing, but that gave me goosebumps'
Oprah Winfrey

to go on Oprah's show to introduce the band. 'We found, I think, some of the best undiscovered operatic singers in the world and asked them to make an album which is classical but at the same time popular. And for me, it was the best thing I had ever heard,' he told Oprah. The band then took centre stage to perform 'Regresa A Mi' and the audience went wild. Oprah herself was blown away: 'I don't know what they were singing, but that gave me goosebumps.'

American fans eager to register their approval and support were soon blogging away, gushing about the band. One fan, Debbie, had been at home sick from work when the show aired and counted her lucky stars she had been. 'I have not been this excited by anything on the music scene for years!' she wrote, adding that Il Divo were both 'thrilling' and 'captivating'. Imani shared her views, explaining that her ears had been opened to a whole new genre of music. She concluded with 'Two thumbs up for these divine performers', a sentiment echoed by many. This was just the first of a slew of shows Il Divo appeared on while on their publicity tour of the States. Within a fortnight of making their US debut on *Oprah* they had also appeared on the *Jay Leno Show*, *Regis and Kelly*, *Today* with Katie Couric and then on *Showbiz Tonight* on 19 April, the day the album was finally released in the USA and in Canada.

If they were wondering what effect all this media coverage would have on record sales they didn't have to wonder for long: by 29 April the album debuted at number four in the Billboard 200 bestsellers chart with first-week sales of 146,000 copies. This was the highest US chart entry for a debut album by a UK-signed band. Even better, it debuted at number one in the US Billboard crossover chart, displacing Josh Groban's *Closer*, which had held the top spot for a massive sixty-eight weeks. It was a brilliant result for the boys; however, they were no longer in the States to savour their success: they had already flown on to Australia to do a ten-day promotional tour of Sydney and Melbourne.

In 1999 David Miller had spent three months living in Sydney while at the Sydney Opera House performing in *The Pearl Fishers*. This time round his arrival, and that of Urs, Carlos and Sébastien, was to attract a much broader audience. The boys could only stand back and watch in amazement as the album shot straight to the number one slot in the ARIA classical chart, refusing to budge for seven weeks, and debuted at number four on the ARIA Top 50 album chart, before working its way to the top slot six weeks later. In front of a crowd of over a thousand fans at Mall Music at the Warringah Mall in Sydney they sang

'Unbreak My Heart', 'My Way' and 'Mama' before signing copies of their album. 'They were gracious, approachable and chatted with the crowd,' noted Philip Spence of the Mall's management team. The crowd, in turn, simply fell in love with the boys, including Berta Cunico, an eighty-one-year-old who had been waiting to see them since 9.30 that morning.

In Melbourne there was yet another prestigious television appearance: the forty-seventh TV Week Logie Awards. Their rendition of 'My Way' wowed a whole new set of fans. With an audience of 2.3 million, if there was anyone Down Under who hadn't heard of Il Divo before this night, they certainly had afterwards.

But it was time for the band to move on again and mid May saw them back in the States, appearing on another TV awards show. Simon Cowell joined the likes of Aretha Franklin, Ellen DeGeneres and Tony Danza in presenting the Daytime Emmy Awards, while Il Divo performed, backed by a live orchestra. 'The romantic overtures of Il Divo's music are a perfect fit with the passion and drama of daytime television,' gushed Al Schwartz, who produced the two-hour TV special of the ceremony. Ellen DeGeneres obviously liked the guys because they then appeared on her daytime talk show alongside *Friends* star Lisa Kudrow.

By June the boys had moved countries again, this time hopping over the border to Canada for a whirlwind press tour, appearing live at First Canadian Place in downtown Toronto to meet fans and sign autographs. *Il Divo*, the album, had by then been in the Canadian Soundscan Top 100 album charts for seven weeks, debuting at number one and never dropping out of the top three, earning double-platinum status.

By the end of June the boys had also managed to fit in fleeting visits to Barcelona, Switzerland, France, Finland and Portugal, but the busiest period since the band's inception was just about to begin. Back in America, the band was able to take part in one of the worthiest undertakings the music business has ever initiated. On the twentieth anniversary of the ground-breaking Live Aid concerts, Sir Bob Geldof and his many influential musician friends put together an extraordinary worldwide series of concerts. Live 8 wanted to send a message to the leaders of G8, the eight wealthiest countries in the world, and the message was a simple one – make poverty history. While U2 were singing live in Hyde Park with Sir Paul McCartney, Il Divo joined the American line up in Philadelphia, performing outside the Museum of Modern Art for an audience in excess of 250,000.

'...these guys have a lot of charisma'
Simon Cowell

Finally, on 4 July, the band were in Washington at America's premier Independence Day event, performing alongside the Beach Boys, the O'Jays and Gloria Estefan, in front of an estimated audience of 400,000. The television audience for this event was a massive 13.5 million.

Now, after all the razzmatazz and hullabaloo of America, it was time for Il Divo to return to the calmer climes of England. They were about to make their first proper full-length live appearance and where better to do that than at the ever-so-civilised Henley Festival, at the finale. They were due to appear at 8.45p.m. on the Floating Stage and by that time all the unreserved seats out front had well and truly been taken by diehard Il Divo fans. They weren't to be disappointed. Suddenly the boys arrived in a vintage, open-top Rolls Royce. Then, accompanied by the Heart of England Chamber Ensemble, they sang to rapturous applause. In case they hadn't already done enough to ensure the life-long devotion of the audience, they then encored with 'Unchained Melody' and had everyone captivated. Their return to England was short and sweet: after the Henley Festival the band departed for Sweden to work on recording their second album, *Ancora*.

By the middle of September they were back in London, at the Royal Albert Hall, for Asda's Tickled Pink (Girls' Night In) concert, a special benefit for breast cancer. Good causes and charities are close to all the band members' hearts but there is one special charity Sébastien supports. This is Assistance Médicale Toit du Monde, which does terrific work in Nepal, Tibet and India helping street children and those affected by poverty, providing basic sanitation and offering medical assistance. Sébastien organised a prize draw to win one of his Armani suits, with all profits from the ticket sales going to the charity. When the draw closed in September it had made £3,543.

It was time for Il Divo to rev up the media merry-go-round again, publicising the next phase in their quest for world domination: the launch of that all-important second album, *Ancora*. Many fans might have felt that after the divine debut, the boys would not be able to reach the same giddy heights again. Il Divo were about to prove them well and truly wrong.

ANCORA

'On the second album, there's going to be a French track, there's going to be some more Spanish, some covers and we might even get around to writing our own piece.' David Miller

The second Il Divo album has a distinctive Spanish and French flavour, with a track listing of eleven songs – including two seasonal favourites, 'O Holy Night' and 'Ave Maria', as well as pop mega-hit 'Unchained Melody'. There is a bonus track for the UK CD: 'Esisti Dentro Me'. Besides tunes such as 'Si Tú Me Amas', 'Hasta Mi Final', 'Pour Que Tu M'Aimes Encore', there are some interesting choices that fans will cherish once they've heard the Il Divo versions.

Track One on *Ancora* is 'Heroe', a Spanish smash hit for Enrique Iglesias (son of Julio), which was also covered by Mariah Carey. Her version sums up the idea that we all have a hero inside us if only we would take the time and trouble to look – a great song for fathers, and a sort of Il Divo 'I Will Survive' track, with its strong self-preservation sentiments, which could be to men what 'Mama' was to mums.

Track Two, 'Isabel', was originally recorded by Luis Miguel, who at one point dated Mariah Carey. Miguel's own style is a sort of Mexican Elvis or Ricky Martin – the Latin boy lover has won three Grammys and received thirty-five platinum records due to a loyal and large fanbase. As he is known for immaculate taste in choosing tunes to cover, it's no surprise that Il Divo wanted to record this beauty in their own style – a torrid, longing song about being in a state of total abandonment, where everything about Isabel becomes a metaphor for love and desire.

Track Three, 'I Believe In You' ('Je Crois En Toi'), was originally supposed to be an Il Divo duet with Canadian singer Céline Dion. At the last moment, the chanteuse's schedule could not be altered to include the time needed to lay down the tune. As Urs said at the time, 'It was a shame, but she was the first name that came up when we discussed the duet so the fact she agreed to do the song is the main thing.' Although Dion did record a tune of a similar name ('Je Crois Toi'), this is not to be confused with the Il Divo track, which was written by René Grignon and Eddy Marnay. Marnay, who died at the age of eighty-two, wrote almost 4,000 tunes for singers the world over but he is probably best known recently for giving Céline Dion her first album, which featured songs exclusively written by him and also such tunes as 'My Friend Left Me' and 'Tellement J'ai D'Amour Pour Toi'. He also penned songs for Françoise Hardy, Claude François, Henri El Salvador and Bourvil as well as Michael Legrand and Nana Mouskouri.

The fourth track, 'Unchained Melody' ('Senza Catene'), has a long and enviable hit history. This is, perhaps, one of Simon Cowell's personal favourites – an old workhorse that pleases crowds wherever it goes. Written by Alex North and Hy Zaret, the song has featured in many movies – in 1978's *Alone in The Dark*, 1983's *Baby It's You* and it more recently found fame for a whole new generation as the musical touchstone in the romantic film *Ghost* (1990) starring Demi Moore and Patrick Swayze. It also made stars of Robson and Jerome, Cowell's first 'put-together' act. The song is remade here, sung in Italian by the divos. One of the reasons why it works is its simplicity, and the combination of four mighty voices does change the timbre of this classic hit.

Cowell has admitted that doing cover versions is always challenging and that the temptation to change the song is always there but, as he has said, 'You have to remember the song was written to be recorded in a certain way. You can leave the audience cold if you try to reinvent the wheel.' According to

'Ancora! Ancora!'

ASCAP, the American music rights society, it was the top love song of the 1950s *and* the 1990s.

According to pianist Ivan Chandler, MD of Musicalities, 'Unchained Melody' has a special place in the pantheon of popular tunes. 'It's a very satisfying song to play and singers always gain a great response from their audiences.' Ivan, who is also a rights expert in the use of music in films, adds that it came from a film called *Unchained* (1955). There wasn't a title for the song as such so it was named 'Unchained Melody'. Jimmy Young, the BBC radio presenter and one-time DJ, had the first UK hit with his version. It was a mega-hit for the Righteous Brothers (who weren't even brothers!) although George Benson knocked out a great cover too. Gareth Gates, Liberace and Leo Sayer have also recorded the tune.

The sixth track is the famous 'Ave Maria', one of the most beautiful classical songs and perhaps one of the most misused. Recorded by artists from Shirley Bassey and Andrea Bocelli to Chris Cornell of Soundgarden (an admirable attempt, which desperately needs drum-machine removal) and The Cranberries. This is a test of any vocalist's ability, as the voice needs to soar and remain flexible, with power needed through the whole range. A weak voice cannot sing this and do it justice so thank heavens there is no such thing in Il Divo. In fact, David, Urs, Carlos and Sébastien all fly through this megawatt test of vocal skill.

Track Eight, 'All By Myself' ('Sola Otra Vez'), is the power ballad that provided a big hit for US singer Eric Carmen, who penned the track, as well as for Céline Dion. One of the most moving songs about loneliness since Gilbert O'Sullivan's 'Alone Again (Naturally)' or Badfinger's 'Without You', this is a powerful track that is relentless in its cry for love. Also, it takes a powerful voice to make the emotions real – hence a perfect, if not inspired choice for the men from Il Divo.

Track Nine is 'En Aranjuez Con Tu Amor', a song about a love that was terminated without good reason but, tantalisingly, could be renewed again. Aranjuez is a town south of Madrid noted as a picturesque setting. The second movement of Joaquin Rodrigo's *Guitar Concerto* (1939), it was played by a flugelhorn solo (under the nickname 'Orange Juice' as that is how the Spanish word sounds to English ears when said quickly) and featured in the Channel 4 film *Brassed Off*. This beautiful and well-loved classic has been covered by Sarah Brightman, Swingle Singers, Andrea Bocelli, Urban Voices, Miles Davis and José Feliciano.

Track Twelve, 'O Holy Night', is a Christmas carol – a classic whose words were written in French in 1847 by Placide Cappeau de Roquemaure. The man was a wine seller but was asked by the local priest to come up with a poem for Christmas. He asked his friend, successful composer Adolphe Charles Adams, to provide some music. It is said to be the very first song broadcast over the airwaves. Translated into English by John Sullivan Dwight, the song has been covered by everyone but most notably by Céline Dion, Mariah Carey, Michael Bolton and Jewel as well as Nat King Cole.

The Il Divo quartet are to open the 2006 World Cup football champion-ships in Germany – and the men are putting voice to a new song to be used as an anthem. According to one recording industry expert, 'Il Divo are perfect to open the cup. They've sold over four million albums and are famous around the world. Hopefully it will become a global anthem for the cup. The boys can sing in different languages so the song will probably not just be in English.'

Il Divo's diva fans from America to Australia are just dying for them to announce the dates of their upcoming world tour, due to take place in 2006. For the many people who have been following the fortunes of the band since that first astonishing appearance on *Parkinson* (or on *Oprah* in the States), it will be the icing on the cake.

For Urs, Sébastien, Carlos and David, it will be the climax of a fantastic journey. Plucked from all over the globe and picked as the best of the best, the boys all had to leave their previous lives behind in order to participate in the phenomenon that is Il Divo. Since then they have rehearsed and sung their hearts out, in the studio, on TV shows and at live events, in order to bring their unique brand of music to people all over the world. In doing so they have won themselves the gratitude and undying devotion of thousands of loyal fans. The forthcoming tour will certainly bring them many more admirers and make them even more popular. And as audiences across the globe rise to their feet, applauding loudly, they'll all be shouting 'Ancora! Ancora!'

PICTURE CREDITS

p. 8 In Central Park, New York, 7 July 2005 (*Big Pictures*)

p. 10 At Henley Festival of Music and the Arts, where the group performed a selection of songs from their album, 10 July 2005 (*Rosie Hartnell/Redferns*)

p. 13 At Capital Radio, Leicester Square, London, for UK Radio Aid, 17 January 2005 (*McCormack/Xposure © Xposure Photo Agency Limited*)

p. 14–15 At the party for the UK gala film premiere of *Bridget Jones: The Edge of Reason*, London, 9 September 2004 (*Dave Hogan/ Getty Images*)

p. 16 Signing album covers at HMV, Toronto, Canada, 17 June 2005 (*Norm Betts/Rex Features*)

p. 18 In Central Park, New York, 7 July 2005 (*Big Pictures*)

p. 21 The band with manager Simon Cowell at Chiswick House, Chiswick Park, July 2004 (*Image supplied courtesy of Hugo Dixon*)

p. 24 David Miller in Amsterdam, July 2005 (*Image supplied courtesy of William Rutten*)

p. 27 Promotional headshot of David Miller, 1998 (*Image supplied courtesy of Washington National Opera*)

p. 28 [Top] David playing the part of Hoffman in *The Tales of Hoffman*, April 2002; [bottom] in the role of Romeo in *Romeo and Juliet* at the Connecticut Opera, October 1998 (*Judith W. Lester*)

p. 29 David starring in the lead role in *Faust* at the Connecticut Opera, April 2001 (*Judith W. Lester*)

p. 32–33 David performing in *West Side Story* at the Teatro alla Scala, Milan, 1999 (*Teatro alla Scala, Milan*)

p. 34 David with Nicole Kidman at the pre-Broadway engagement of Baz Lurhman's *La Bohème*, October 2002 (*Lyn Hughes/ WireImage.com*)

p. 39 David at the Thirty-Second Annual Daytime Emmy Awards, held at the Radio City Music Hall, New York, 20 May 2005 (*John Stanton/Getty Images*)

p. 41 David on *Cilla Live* for Living TV, London, 19 December 2004 (*Ken McKay/Rex Features*)

p. 42–43 Nordoff-Robbins Christmas Carol Concert, 20 December 2004 (*Dave M Benett/Getty Images*)

p. 44 Sébastien in Amsterdam, July 2005 (*Image supplied courtesy of William Rutten*)

p. 52 Sébastien during a visit to the *Today* show with Simon Cowell, 18 April 2005 (*Film Magic*)

p. 55 Sébastien appearing on *Cilla Live* for Living TV, London, 19 December 2004 (*Ken McKay/Rex Features*)

p. 58–59 At the UK gala film premiere of *Bridget Jones: The Edge of Reason* at the Odeon Cinema, Leicester Square, London, 9 September 2004 (*Nikki Black/Xposure © Xposure Photo Agency Limited*)

p. 60 Urs Buhler in Amsterdam, July 2005 (*Image supplied courtesy of William Rutten*)

p. 63 Rehearsal for *Les Troyens* by Hector Berlioz at the Dutch Opera, 30 September 2003 (*Werry Crone/Hollandse Hoogte*)

p. 64 Urs at the UK gala film premiere of *Bridget Jones: The Edge of Reason* at the Odeon Cinema, Leicester Square, London, 9 September 2004 (*Nikki Black/Xposure © Xposure Photo Agency Limited*)

p. 67 Urs Buhler at an instore appearance, 24 April 2005 (*John Stanton/Getty Images*)

p. 70 Urs at an Il Divo instore appearance, 24 April 2005 (*John Stanton/Getty Images*)

p. 73 Urs appearing on *Cilla Live* for Living TV, London, 19 December 2004 (*Ken McKay/Rex Features*)

p. 74–75 Il Divo perform during the Thirty-Second Annual Daytime Emmy Awards held at Radio City Music Hall, New York, 20 May 2005 (*Scott Gries/Getty Images*)

p. 76 Carlos Marin in Amsterdam, July 2005 (*Image supplied courtesy of William Rutten*)

p. 78 Carlos as Teen Angel singing 'Beauty School Drop-Out' in a production of *Grease* at the Teatro Lope de Vega, Madrid, 1999 (*Nacho Arias Careaga*)

p. 80 Carlos in the opera *La Magia de Broadway* [*The Magic of Broadway*] with popular Spanish singer Marta Sáanchez, Lara Theatre, Madrid, 2001 (*Nacho Arias Careaga*)

p. 81 Carlos as the Beast in *Beauty and the Beast* at the Teatro Lope de Vega, Madrid, 1998 (*Nacho Arias Careaga*)

p. 85 Carlos at an Il Divo instore appearance, 24 April 2005 (*John Stanton/Getty Images*)

p. 86 Carlos at the UK gala film premiere of *Bridget Jones: The Edge of Reason* at the Odeon Cinema, Leicester Square, London, 9 September 2004 (*Nikki Black/Xposure © Xposure Photo Agency Limited*)

p. 89 Carlos appearing on *Cilla Live* for Living TV, London, 19 December 2004 (*Ken McKay/ Rex Features*)

p. 92 Carlos at an Il Divo instore appearance, 24 April 2005 (*John Stanton/Getty Images*)

p. 94–95 Il Divo arrive at the Thirty-Second Annual Daytime Emmy Awards held at Radio City Music Hall, New York, 20 May 2005 (*Nancy Kaszerman/ZUMA/Corbis*)

p. 98 Filming their first video for 'Regressa A Mi' in Slovenia, September 2004 (*Camera Press/Ken Rake*)

p. 101 Il Divo instore appearance, 24 April 2005 (*John Stanton/Getty Images*)

p. 104–105 Il Divo instore appearance, 24 April 2005 (*John Stanton/Getty Images*)

p. 108 Appearing on *Cilla Live* for Living TV, London, 19 December 2004 (*Ken McKay/Rex Features*)

p. 112–113 Il Divo perform during the Fête de la Musique at Versailles Palace (*Stéphane Reix/Fête de la musique/France 2/For Picture/ Corbis*)

p. 114 The boys in Paris (*Empics*)

p. 118–119 Appearing on *Cilla Live* for Living TV, London, 19 December 2004 (*Ken McKay/ Rex Features*)

p. 120 At the Asda Tickled Pink performance, London, 18 September 2005 (*Hertz/Xposure © Xposure Photo Agency Limited*)

p. 122 At the Oxford Street Christmas lights ceremony, 15 November 2004 (*Film Magic*)

p. 126–127 At the party for the UK gala film premiere of *Bridget Jones: The Edge of Reason*, London, 9 September 2004 (*David Westing/Getty Images*)

With thanks to Annabel Merullo for picture research.